D0254675

"When you walk onto Jay Billy's campus, you immediately know every single student and staff member matters. From the excitement on the playground to the crazy hats Jay wears while greeting students, you sense right away that his school is the place the whole community wants to be. In *Lead with Culture*, you will be taken on a journey of how a one of a kind principal built a culture full of love with all hands on deck. Jay will also take you through his own personal stories as an educator who holds growth, staying current, and being a PIRATE leader as priorities. You will learn the *how* to Jay's *why* every step of the way. Each chapter is exploding with ideas for making your school culture better, as well as questions and challenges that will push you to think deeply and take action. Jay also shares his struggles and how he overcame them, which keep his stories real and relatable. This is a book that welcomes the reader with open arms. You will feel a part of Jay's community and come away inspired to make an impact."

—Nili Bartley, technology integration specialist, Hopkinton School District, Hopkinton, Massachusetts

"Jay Billy is the type of school leader every child deserves. In his book, he lays it all out there, everything that goes into building a positive culture in your school, leading like a PIRATE, and connecting with each and every student, colleague, and family member. By sharing great personal experiences and practical ideas, Jay shows us the way to make our schools great! Yes, *culture matters*. The best way to make it matter in your school is to start with this book!"

—Rich Czyz, author of *Four O'Clock Faculty*, principal, Thomas Richards School, New Jersey

"In this school-culture leadership gem, Jay Billy calls upon years of experience and connection to help caregivers polish what matters in our school climate. Who better to know, after all, about what's really important in a school than the lead learner? Treasure the engaging stories and practical strategies of this veteran principal. Mine his creative ideas to empower students and staff alike to shine big and bright. Intentionally plant, nurture, stretch, grow, and cultivate those seeds of inspiration and greatness. Then excavate the nuggets of wisdom and warmth in this must-have guidebook and enjoy the sparkle in your character building."

—**Barbara Gruener,** school counselor and
author of *What's Under Your Cape?*

"Throughout the pages of *Lead with Culture*, you will feel passion oozing through the spaces of every word and every line. 'You can't fake passion,' and Jay Billy does not disappoint when practicing this principle. He shares many ideas to help educators create a culture where "we make learning a side effect and the love of learning the goal.

"Jay not only helps us recognize that everything we do matters, but he encourages us to chart our own culture building course. From wearing silly hats, making a ruckus, saying 'YES' to teachers, and sharing 'Golden Hearted' relationships with the entire school community, Jay inspires the reader to discover meaningful ways to navigate the seas of building a positive school culture.

"Stop waiting! Dive in! In short order, you will be inspired to create cultural change in your system."

—**Tara Martin,** author of *Be REAL,* coordinator,
Auburn Washburn USD 437, Kansas

"Sincere. Open. Honest. Moving forward. Administrators in education will find Jay Billy's book inspiring and purposeful in cultivating a positive school climate in ways that will support and challenge their staff, their students, and the families that enter their school building each day. *Lead with Culture* will remind educators that following their passions, smiling a lot, and having fun are necessary key elements when it comes to leading like a pirate."

—**Darlene Farrace-Prott,** professional development consultant, author, New Jersey Teacher to Teacher, LLC

"Inspiration begins with Jay's opening remarks and never leaves the reader's imagination throughout the book. *Lead with Culture* is a call to action that encourages every school leader, regardless of title or position, to search and tap into the greatness that can be found in every student, paraprofessional, teacher, parent, and community stake-holder. Each chapter ends with challenges that ignite the most important skill an educator can harness, *reflection*. Well before you finish the last paragraph, on that last page, you will be chanting, 'Why not? Let's do it!' And when you put the book down, you'll probably be teary-eyed with hope and inspiration because no matter what tomorrow brings to your district, school, or classroom, you'll be fueled by the guidance and permission Principal Billy has given you to 'be brave,' to be you, to be simply awesome! One word of caution: School will never be the same for you once you've embraced the tenets of *Lead with Culture*."

—**Richard W. Allen, EdS,** retired principal, cofounder of DisruptED TV, adjunct professor NJPSA Monmouth University, Leadership Academy Presenter, NJ DOE ELC Member

"*Lead with Culture* is an excellent guide for exploring what really matters in schools. Jay Billy has been a role model as a teacher and administrator because he exudes culture and develops relationships by being real. The book is an easy read because he captures the essence of education. Culture, expectations, learning, thinking, enthusiasm, and joy all matter. The book addresses relationships, community, and being connected. Infused throughout are the soft skills that Mr. Billy demonstrates daily.

"Jay kindly mentions his relationship with the Pre-Teachers at Rider University with whom he gives his time and energy. Our students are better because they work with Jay and are part of his professional learning network (PLN). This spirit of giving, building relationships, and driving home of the message that #KindnessMatters pervades his writing.

"A key thread that runs through the book is Jay's eagerness to celebrate culture. Whether it is welcoming kids as they get off the bus, recognizing faculty and staff, taking kids outside when it snows, his actions are purposeful, exciting, and passionate.

"One need only spend a few hours delving into Jay's journey to understand what really matters in school and how each of his topics can benefit the reader daily. *Lead with Culture* is a must read for all who love education."

—Michael G. Curran Jr., EdD, professor of Teacher Education, Rider University, Lawrenceville, New Jersey

"District leaders, school leaders, teacher leaders, and educators of every kind, stop what you're doing and read this book! In *Lead with Culture*, Jay Billy takes creating a positive climate and culture to a new level. You will read about a transformational leader who unfailingly walks the walk and makes every effort to convey his high expectations of himself, his staff, and his students. We all know how easy it is to become swept up in the minutia of day-to-day meetings, requirements, and obligations that cause us to lose sight of what really matters. Reading this book provided me with ideas about how to up my game, make a meaningful impact in unique and powerful ways, and to dig deep and employ engaging strategies that really matter to the people who matter most. Jay Billy's candor regarding his own imperfections in dealing with issues in the past help his readers to relate to him and feel secure in their own quest to know better and do better. Thanks for *Leading with Culture* and showing us how to do it too, Jay Billy!"

—**Pamela Hernandez,** principal, John F. Kennedy
Elementary School, New Jersey

A *LEAD* Like a PIRATE *Guide*

LEAD with

CULTURE

What Really MATTERS in Our Schools

Jay Billy

LEAD with CULTURE

© 2018 by Jay Billy

This book is available at special discounts when purchased in quantity for use as premiums, promotions, fundraisers, or for educational use. For inquiries and details, contact the publisher at books@daveburgessconsulting.com.

Published by Dave Burgess Consulting, Inc.
San Diego, CA
DaveBurgessConsulting.com

Cover Design by Genesis Kohler
Editing and Interior Design by My Writers' Connection

Library of Congress Control Number: 2018942305
Paperback ISBN: 978-1-946444-79-0
Ebook ISBN: 978-1-946444-80-6

First Printing: May 2018

DEDICATION

This book is dedicated to my children: Samantha, Michael, Delaney, Logan, and Fallon. You are the reason for all that I do. I couldn't ask for a greater, more loving group of kids. Somehow you all turned out okay, despite having me as your dad.

It's also dedicated to my parents, who taught me the value of hard work, loved me unconditionally, and reminded me that one of the most important things a parent can do is just be there. Thanks, Mom and Dad. Miss you, Mom!

CONTENTS

FOREWORD

by Beth Houf and Shelley Burgess

Life as an educational leader can be lonely. When you take on an administrative role, your task list multiplies, and time seems to evaporate. A strong network of support—to celebrate the great things happening as well as get you through those rough moments—is essential for your success. We wrote *Lead Like a PIRATE* to provide that support. We wanted to encourage and equip educators by sharing our stories and strategies. We wanted to be sure that no one felt as if he or she was alone. Our goal has been to set up systems of support through our professional learning networks (PLN) to empower leaders to take risks to ensure that school is an amazing place for both students and staff.

Since our book's release, we have been inspired as we've watched the #LeadLAP crew grow. The examples and stories shared daily on our hashtag made us realize that we are surrounded by greatness. One evening after our book was published, we started brainstorming how we could continue to support leaders in a way that wasn't the norm. One thing we discussed was the fact that leaders sometimes get overwhelmed by the amount of information that is being shared at what seems like lightning speed. How might we offer bite-size expertise for leaders that would have huge impact on schools? The *Lead Like a PIRATE* Guides were born.

We are honored to introduce our very first of the *Lead Like a PIRATE Guides: Lead with Culture: What Really Matters in Our Schools* by Jay Billy. Jay is constantly inspiring and motivating by showcasing the incredible things that are happening at Slackwood Elementary in Lawrence, New Jersey, where he serves as building principal. Jay shares his stories of successes and failures along the course of building a school culture that definitely gets students, staff, parents, and the community running in each and every day. Jay also highlights strategies that he has learned from others, magnifying the core belief that we are always better together. Jay walks the talk and has a way of inspiring and motivating to bring out the best in us all. The mission of culture first, culture next, culture always comes alive on the pages that follow in practical and life changing ways.

As we noted in *Lead Like a PIRATE*, PIRATE leadership is about being the kind of leaders we always wanted to be and creating the kinds of schools we dream of for kids. Pirate leaders relentlessly search for ways to make school amazing for students and staff. These leaders don't simply believe schools can be better; they *know* schools can be better and will stop at nothing to make it happen. Jay Billy is a PIRATE leader in every way, and we are honored to have him as part of our crew.

In the spirit of always working towards greatness and knowing that learning never ends, here is our first book of many that will help to provide inspiration and leadership ideas for all that are doing this most important work. Thank you for your dedication to making school an amazing place.

Lead Like a PIRATE

Passion

Pirate leaders bring their passion to work. They also work to identify and bring out the passions of their staff members and students.

Immersion

Pirate leaders are immersed in their work and relationships which enables them to make an impact on those they lead.

Rapport

Pirate leaders intentionally build trust and rapport with the entire crew.

Ask and Analyze

Pirate leaders ask great questions and engage in meaningful conversations that empower people to take risks.

Transformation

Pirate leaders transform the mundane into the spectacular. They make essentials, such as staff meetings and professional development training, engaging and effective.

Enthusiasm

Pirate leaders are enthusiastic and positive. They work to create an environment where teachers and students are excited about coming to school each day.

My Story

I didn't grow up wanting to be a principal or even a teacher. My first love was sports and coaching. I was always the guy who wanted to be the best no matter what I was doing. I was willing to work longer hours, sleep less, and go above and beyond in my quest for greatness. When my wrestling career ended after college in 1983, I set my focus on coaching. As a wrestling coach, it took me a long time to figure out that not all my athletes got into their sports with the same dedication to excellence. I couldn't understand it. Why didn't they care as much about their performance as I did? Why did I feel more pain when they lost than it seemed they felt themselves? I felt so frustrated with some of my athletes because I wanted more for them. Hoping that one day their drive would kick in, I pushed them as hard as I could. I didn't want them to waste their talents.

Step ahead twenty-plus years, after college wrestling and coaching, after being a principal in other districts and starting programs as a principal and a supervisor. I am now a proud principal of a small elementary school in New Jersey. I have had the opportunity to teach at the college and high school level and supervise at both the secondary and elementary levels for many years, and that fire for excellence still burns within me. I want the best for my kids and my staff. Average isn't an option because what I do is not a job; it's a passion.

When I pushed my wrestlers to their limits as a coach, I didn't think of what I was doing in terms of building culture or relationships. My goal was to keep getting better—as individuals and as a team. That is still my goal. I don't believe there is room for average in education; we must hold ourselves, our colleagues, and our students to the highest of standards. To pull the greatness out of our students, we must first see it in them and then nurture it. That's how we make school a place where miracles can happen.

In 2013 I came across the book *Teach Like a PIRATE* by Dave Burgess. Later that year, I had the honor of watching him speak at a workshop for teachers. Seeing Dave on stage changed everything for me. I had always considered myself as good at my job, but I also felt "buttoned up"—uncomfortable sharing my fun and silly side. Dave gave me permission to do whatever is necessary to create experiences for our students. His discussion about making presentation a key area of the entire lesson—in addition to content and pedagogy—as well as his refusal to accept the excuse that "It's easy for you, you're creative" (an excuse I had used many times), made it possible for me to step well beyond average. For years I had kept so many great ideas (and laughs) inside, and that day, Dave encouraged me to let loose! After attending his workshop, I began using the Ask/Analyze tactic for every lesson and for every meeting I planned. Suddenly I was free to try to make students laugh, share my passions, entertain people, and keep them guessing. I try to put a smile on everyone's face. I share this side of me with the students, the staff, and the families. I push hard, sometimes too hard, but it's all for the kids. It has been an amazing journey for me and those with whom I work who choose to come along. Thank you ahead of time for choosing to read about my journey and sharing my passion for the greatest profession in the world!

CULTURE MATTERS

PIRATE leaders infuse enthusiasm into their work.
They bring it every day, and they are committed to
being on. They are the champions and cheerleaders
of their schools and champions and cheerleaders of
those who work and learn there.

—Lead Like a PIRATE

In my first years as a principal, I was afraid of the teachers who were so good and innovative—the kinds of teachers we all wish our kids had. These teachers had established a culture where everyone knew their class was *the* place to be. They always did that "something extra" that made their class special and made kids excited about being in school. They consistently performed with both uniqueness and excellence with little regard for what their peers were doing or thinking. I was afraid of them because they had a reputation for greatness.

Let me explain.

Each year as it came time to place students for the next year, I worried about who would get the "star" teacher's students and how those parents would react to a new teacher who may be less innovative, communicative, and stellar. I worried about whom I would place in the "star" teacher's classroom for the upcoming year, and often I based my decisions on the parents' visibility and involvement. In some ways, I despised how good these teachers were because of the anxiety these decisions caused me, not to mention the task of explaining my reasoning to parents. As we all know, parents talk, and everyone wanted their kids in those teachers' classes.

It later occurred to me that I needed to create a buzz about my other teachers. More than that, I needed them to step up their games and create a culture of excitement and possibility about their classes the way my "star" teachers had done. It wasn't my job to hide the success of the school's best teachers; my job was to celebrate their greatness and help others find their own greatness. This is the culture that I wanted for my school, and to get it, I needed to be a better leader.

Understanding that I needed to create a culture where excellence was the norm and where people felt challenged and encouraged to constantly improve, I watched and learned from my best teachers. In talking with them, I encouraged them to lead by sharing their best ideas. I also learned about others who were doing great things, and I shared their stories. The ultimate goal, of course, was to help *all* our teachers get better and in doing so, make our school amazing.

Learning, listening, sharing, and *leading* started the change that was necessary for our school to be a place of learning and excitement. I changed as a leader as I sought to empower greatness in my staff. No longer was I worried about where I was going to place the students from the "star" teacher's classroom, because I had many star teachers. Each had built a culture of growth and learning and love in their classrooms. They were unique and different, and they all had their specific skills. By cultivating greatness within the individual teachers, our *school*'s culture changed. It became the place everyone—our staff, students, and their families—wanted to be.

Culture, in its most basic sense, is "the way we do things around here." A school's culture, which leads to the climate, determines "the way it feels" when anyone walks into the building or the classroom. Culture exists whether we are intentional about creating it or not, but it's a *positive culture* that is essential to making the necessary changes within our schools. Change is a constant factor in our schools, and because that's true, culture is never stagnant. Each decision that is made, each new staff member who joins an organization, each mandate from the state brings a slight shift in culture. As leaders, our responsibility to the children in our schools is to give them the best education possible, and that happens when we drive a culture of learning and positive strength.

We should all strive to create schools where, as, Beth Houf and Shelley Burgess say,"...students and staff are knocking doors down to get in rather than out."[1] We want schools to be a feel-good place where everyone feels safe to be themselves and where learning is a priority for all. We want a climate of excitement and enthusiasm. We want to be the place that people talk about and remember. We want to be the place where everyone in the community wants their kids and grandkids to be. That's the culture we strive for.

Pass It On

In this book, I will be sharing things that I used or have seen used to make classrooms and schools great places. As I tell my teachers, "Every recommendation I give, I've learned from someone else or somewhere else." I didn't make this stuff up; I've learned from so many people. I'm simply sharing ideas with the hope of helping you—and school leaders everywhere—develop the kind of culture that brings out the best in staff and students.

At the end of each chapter, you'll find some activity questions to get you thinking deeper about this amazing profession we are in. Please share what you've learned and experienced at #LeadLAP.

Leadership Treasure Hunt
(Find This)

What would you say is the current culture of your school or your classroom? How do you know?

Navigating the Seas
(Think about This)

What would be the first thing you changed in your school to change the culture in a positive way?

Charting the Course
(Take Action)

Make it a point to smile more and say hello to each student and staff member who walks in; in fact, be more welcoming in all ways.

Share your thoughts and ideas!
#LeadLAP

EXPECTATIONS MATTER

You never actually arrive at greatness; it's a moving target, a lifelong pursuit.
—Lead Like a PIRATE

When I started at my current school in 2011, I was informed that about 60 percent of the students in our Title 1 school came from homes where English was not the primary language. Research indicates students who leave third grade without the ability to read at grade level have a significantly lower chance of graduating from high school and moving on to college. Knowing this, I searched for information about schools that had succeeded despite the socioeconomic and language factors, and the resource that paved the way was a book by Jeff King and Damen Lopez titled *Turnaround Schools: Creating Cultures of Universal Achievement*. The book highlights the fact that high expectations are the first requirement for creating a culture of universal achievement. The authors talk about being tenacious and courageous even when things get tough and don't look so good. They also discuss that one of the first steps to achieving your vision is to claim what it is that you expect.[1] As Abraham Lincoln said, "Determine that the thing can and shall be done, and then we shall find the way."[2] I felt inspired to make our school the school people talked about. The school people wanted their children in. The one that made a difference for these children.

At the beginning of the year, our superintendent held a meeting of administrators where we all (there are seven schools in my district) were asked to create our school SMART goal—goals that would be considered in our evaluations. (SMART standing for Specific, Measurable, Attainable, Realistic, and Time Bound.) Knowing the needs of our school and understanding the research, we set this goal: *Every student at Slackwood School will, without exception, be reading at grade level based on the Fountas and Pinnell leveling system by the time they leave third grade.* When I read this aloud in a room full of central office personnel, principals, and district supervisors, my colleagues all looked at me a little sideways. But they know me, so they understood.

The State Department of Education (DOE) had sent some people to this meeting to observe our process, and the first one to question me was a woman from that office: "You can't say that! You know you are being evaluated on this goal, don't you?"

"Yes, we can; and yes, we do. How can we not say that, knowing the research on not reaching the goal?" I responded.

"Well, let's be a little more realistic, based on last years' results," she said.

Now, I'm not stupid. I knew that it was unlikely that all students would be able to reach that goal, especially knowing where they were coming from, but I refused to relent. I asked, "Which students should I pick who won't reach the goal? How can I look at these kids and say,

'You and you, oh . . . and you are not going to be reading at grade level and therefore may not have a successful schooling experience?"

I'm sure the conversations didn't end there, and I know the DOE lady had something to say about me to my superintendent, but I just couldn't say it out loud. I couldn't say that there was a good chance, based on data from previous years, that 30 percent of my students wouldn't reach grade-level proficiency in reading. I also know that if I kept saying the goal out loud to my staff enough, they'd get the importance of pushing to reach it. They'd understand their role in making this goal happen.

Was this goal realistically achievable? It was unlikely, based on history. But, I thought, if every staff member set this as their goal, we had a chance. We couldn't look at ourselves or our students and not try. I know each and every one of my students and I couldn't honestly look at them and say, "You are the one who won't get there."

Motivational speaker Norman Vincent Peale's popular quote is appropriate here: "Shoot for the moon. Even if you miss, you'll land among the stars." When a teacher takes a risk and it works out, I hear things like "I didn't think I could do that." When kids take control of their own learning, I am privileged to witness their teachers sit in awe as they watch their class evolve. If you don't believe amazing things can happen when you try something different, if you aren't willing to take that leap of faith, you are destined to mediocrity—and your students are too. High expectations among *all* members of an organization and a belief in the people—all of the people—is how you grow toward greatness.

> *High expectations among all members of an organization and a belief in the people—all of the people—is how you grow toward greatness.*

9

When you walk into a classroom, you can see the expectations a teacher has for her students by the structures she has set up for students to succeed, and not only succeed but to flourish and achieve far more than many had expected. Hattie's research (evidencebasedteaching.org.au/hatties-2017-updated-list) shows teacher expectations have an effect size of 0.43. Basically, you get what you expect. If you have high expectations, you are giving your students the chance to achieve greatly. If you have low expectations, it's pretty much guaranteed your students will struggle. Having high expectations is more than just words. Teachers must show they expect high levels of learning in every conversation they have and every assignment they give and that their students will respond. Feedback and a focus on learning—not just teaching—are essential in showing students the expectations of the class and the school. This is the same for school leaders. If we have high expectations for our teachers and our students, they will respond, and amazing things can happen. In *Teach Like a Pirate*, Dave Burgess says, "Provide an uncommon experience for your students, and they will reward you with uncommon effort and attitude." The same goes for our teachers. We as leaders must model the "uncommon experiences" we expect our teacher to deliver whether it is in staff meetings, professional development, or on a daily basis in our interactions with our school community.

To end the story about 100 percent of our students reaching their grade level expectations in reading . . . we failed. But we failed forward. We started the year with 63 percent of our third grades reading at their expected level, and we ended with just over 70 percent achieving grade-level expectations. It wasn't the 100 percent we wanted, but by having high expectations, we were able to push another few kids past their previous marks.

One more story about high expectations. In the spring of 2017, I was lucky enough to attend the ASCD Empower 17 conference in Anaheim, California. Garrett Reisman, a retired NASA astronaut who spent time on the International Space Station, was the keynote. He is currently working for Elon Musk and Space X, and at the conference he talked about the work he was doing for them. Obviously I became intrigued with the whole concept of a Mission to Mars. Dr. Reisman talked about the fact that his team has a goal—one that no one believes. But the people at Space X can *see* it. They *feel* it in their bones, and they *expect* to achieve the goal within their lifetime. The best part of Reisman's presentation was when he showed some of their current work—things no one had imagined or thought of before, such as bringing a rocket back to earth and landing it so it can be used again. These creative and previously unheard-of ideas for space flight and landing that Mr. Reisman offered were inspiring and innovative and most of all, exemplified what we talk about in education when we talk about having high expectations for our schools. We must dream of a better and different world. To do this, we must create schools that aren't like they were fifty years ago—not even five years ago. We must think differently because the world is different. Most of all, we must continue to push the envelope of innovation so our children can understand they are the future.

Be Inspired

Check out the Launch and Landing of Falcon Nine by SpaceX here:

bit.ly/FalconLands

Ideas and examples for showing that Expectations Matter:

- **Model it!** You can't hold others to high expectations if you don't have them for yourself. If you have an expectation that teachers will make positive phone calls home, you should be making phone calls too. If you have an expectation that the cleanliness of the school is everyone's responsibility, people should see you cleaning tables and picking up trash.

- **Develop a school mantra or slogan and share it!** Include your school's motto as part of your email signature. Post it around the school. Put it on every meeting document and on your newsletters. The goal is to make sure everyone—parents, staff, teachers, and students—knows what your school's mission or focus is.

- **Make sure you know your community members' hopes and dreams.** Have your teachers share their hopes and dreams with you—their dreams not only for the children but for themselves as learners. At back-to-school night, have parents share their hopes and dreams for their children. Post these goals in a visible location. Make sure everyone knows the expectations for your school!

- **Carefully read and analyze teachers' personal development plans (PDPs).** In New Jersey and in many other states, each teacher must submit a PDP along with the goals and activities they will use to achieve it. Although it takes time, it's important to carefully read these plans. These should guide the teachers in their professional learning quests throughout the year. Each year, during the summative evaluation, I write goals and ideas for the next year. Make sure those are included in each teacher's plan.

- **Make sure you follow through**. If you tell someone you're going to do something, do it. Everyone is watching. To set a high bar, you need to show everyone what is expected and model those expectations yourself.
- **Inspect what you expect.** Make sure to check in daily with your staff to ensure everyone maintains the high level of teaching and learning you expect.

Setting high expectations and then demonstrating those expectations for your staff and students on a daily basis helps people understand your expectations. More importantly, when teachers see you model what it means to live out those high expectations, they will model *their* high expectations for the students.

Culture Matters: Set Expectations

As a school leader, I want to foster a "no excuses" brand of teaching, one that empowers and enables our students to go places they haven't yet imagined. I want to see teachers going deep, not allowing just surface learning. That means establishing a classroom expectation that simple yes/no answers will require more explanation and that students are expected to develop their own questions. When I see my first-grade kids discussing high-level scientific principles, or I see my second graders teaching teachers from another state how to use Mystery Skype in the classroom, that's when I know my teachers get it. When kids are doing things that even their parents and teachers didn't imagine before the year started, that's when I know we've accomplished something. Although our work is never done, we want to keep raising the bar, so our kids are challenged and learn to love learning.

Leadership Treasure Hunt
(Find This)

Find one teacher in your school who never thought he or she would graduate from college and become a teacher but did so because someone believed in him or her.

Navigating the Seas
(Think about This)

Think of a time when you publicly stated a desire or goal that no one (not even you) really believed was possible, and then you (and/or your team) made it happen. Why do you think this was able to happen when no one thought it could be done?

Charting the Course
(Take Action)

How are you going to raise the bar in your school or classroom?

Share your thoughts and ideas!
#LeadLAP

3

LEARNING AND THINKING MATTER

Immersed leaders constantly read books, articles, blog posts, and other literature in an effort to stay current on effective practices and ideas . . . . Truly immersed leaders will be at the table with their team, soaking up and contributing to the learning.

—Lead Like a PIRATE

I'm "that" principal: the one who continually emails staff with new links and ideas I find on Twitter, educators' blogs, and at conferences. I know I drive my teachers a little crazy with all the ideas, but I can't help myself. Thankfully, my teachers "get me," and (some) even appreciate the way I get so excited about cool ideas that could push the boundaries on learning. They know that when I see something I think will be amazing, I *need* to share it. I can't pass up a great teaching idea! So I share, and then I watch and see who is interested in trying something new—who is willing to take a risk to make learning better—to make school amazing.

Sometimes staff members will try an idea the next day. Sometimes I'll see the idea in action the following week or maybe a month later. Every once in a while, I'll share an idea in a meeting that I shared a year or two earlier because no one has implemented it in the classroom—yet. I keep sharing because I want to drive my teachers to be better—and to ensure that our students are becoming the best citizens they can be. Most of all, I share because one of the main reasons school exists is to help our children grow as learners and thinkers.

Yes, teaching is important, but it is the *learning* and *thinking* that really matter. As school leaders, it's up to us to make sure our teachers follow curricular guidelines that are aligned to goals of the nation and the community. We must set the expectation that our students will continually forge ahead in their learning of concepts and material. But it is also our responsibility to make sure teachers and students feel empowered to go off script. We also must create an environment where the teachers think of themselves as learners and are not afraid to take chances and ask questions that push learning and teaching to the next level.

Educational leader and author Brad Currie said it best: "Students take risks when they see teachers take risks. Teachers take risks when they see school leaders take risks." This is so true. If we don't model risk-taking for our teachers, how can we expect them to understand and replicate the growth we wish to see? That means, as leaders, we need to take risks: Try something new in staff meetings. Read an educational book and try a new tech idea. Share ideas you find on Twitter with your teachers and watch to see which ones are using them in their classrooms—and then celebrate their bold choices.

Teach Like a PIRATE (TLAP) Day is one of the risk-taking ideas I saw on Twitter. I saw some schools doing it and reached out to principal Ryan McLane, coauthor of *Your School Rocks . . . So Tell People*. He gave me hints and tips for how to do it, and I was able to take his advice and promote TLAP Day to my staff. Teach Like a PIRATE Day is a day designed around the thought, *"If your students didn't have to be there, would you be teaching to an empty room?"* Teachers develop activities based on passion, either theirs or their students, and students get to choose to come. When I first brought up the idea, the first objection was, "We don't have time for this." This day outside standardized teaching protocols (or in our case, just part of the day) wasn't something they were comfortable with, and they definitely were not excited to get out of their comfort zones. Slowly, people came to the idea. It helped that I told them they had the freedom to work collaboratively or on their own. Most of the teachers decided to join with their grade-level partners and came up with ideas that matched their passions outside of school. Thus, the first Slackwood Teach Like a PIRATE Day was born.

Our TLAP Day, which we held one afternoon after our lunch periods ended, caused quite a bustle in our building. Teachers planned activities like gymnastics, baseball, and crafts. One teacher, whose passion is reading and books, set up a classroom with a variety of books and genres that the students could come to and just find a comfortable seat and read. Kids moved from room to room trying out activities they hadn't done before. Some chose the quiet of the reading room. Others went to different grade-level areas and joined students with whom they had never worked. It was awesome, if I say so myself. The kids had a great time. I heard many students telling their friends, "That was the best day ever!" as they walked to their buses at the end of the day. Even the teachers had fun planning and participating in the activities. We have since held many TLAP Days, and I've even gotten some central office people to run sessions. One of our guest presenters was my superintendent. She's a former chemistry teacher and ran a forensic lab where students had to use real clues to solve a case. Again . . . *awesome!*

Creating a Culture of Universal Achievement

Creating the "Culture of Universal Achievement" that King and Lopez talk about in *Turnaround Schools* begins when we are willing to ask ourselves questions that push our schools toward excellence:

- Do we truly believe that all children can achieve?
- Are we willing to set huge goals, such as making sure all our students can read at grade level by the time they leave our schools?
- Are we continuing the focus on social emotional learning in secondary schools that we started in the elementary grades?
- Are we keeping students excited about learning and asking questions?
- How do we meet the rigorous curricular challenges and keep the students excited about school and learning?
- How do we help them be curious when there's calculus to be learned?

Engaged learning and thinking seems to happen sometimes in spite of the demands on schools—rather than because of them; for example, standardized testing has taken some of the joy out of teaching and learning. Timelines dictate learning and force us to make judgments about what students should be able to do by the time they're eight or fourteen. Doing well on the test is the focus, but we also know that, often, learning ends once the grade is given. When we "teach to the test," our students learn to work only as hard as necessary to get the grade instead of just trying to get better.

I understand the need to measure learning and growth, but in doing so, we unintentionally separate measurable outcomes from many of the important things that naturally happen in joyful schools.

In joyful schools, teachers are passionate about creating good citizens and supporting students to find their passions. When we help children find their passions and we support creativity, we make learning a side effect and the love of learning the goal. The good news is that we can have it all. We can have joyful schools where kids are interested in learning and still able to pass the test. At the same time, it's important to remember that while we can (and should) set high expectations and believe each child has a gift, not every child is gifted in the same way. Or as Dr. Donald Ambrose put it at the Gifted Education and Creativity Symposium at Rider University, "Not all students are gifted in all areas." Acknowledging that truth allows us to use their gifts to create schools that are focused on learning rather than only grades. When schools give voice and choice to our students to learn and develop their strengths, our schools' culture improves, and we *all* become better.

Use Data to Improve Learning and Thinking

Successful schools find ways to track and measure achievement without neglecting personalized learning. They collect and analyze data to improve instruction with the understanding that data analysis is a learning process that isn't just about the numbers. Numbers show us academic and behavioral trends but don't tell the whole story. I could spend days (although I never seem to have that much time) immersed in data regarding reading and writing and math scores, analyzing the information to discover where our students are as learners and where they need to continue to grow and learn.

The numbers are helpful for finding areas for needed improvement, but what these assessments don't show is how a student is thinking. We have fed them information over the years, and they are now spitting that information back to us as best they can. I like the data, but I also like to get to know the students as thinkers. To do that, we must talk to the students and ask questions that do not have yes or no answers. We must listen to the students and allow them to express their passions. Data is great. Students who can think are better! Thinkers are the ones who want to change the world. They are the ones who see a problem and work to fix it to make the world a better place. The more we get to know about our students and how they think, the more we can find out about what they are interested in and the more we can draw out their strengths and passions.

The Learning Never Stops

Another aspect of creating a culture of universal achievement is to model learning for our staff members and our students. Leaders can never stop learning. When I was thirty-eight, I accepted my first principal position at the Joseph Cappello School, a school for special-needs students ages three to eight. Prior to that, I had worked almost extensively in the secondary level as a teacher, coach, supervisor, and vice principal. I say this with all candor: I was not qualified to be the principal of that school. The principal had abruptly left, and I was working right across the street at the high school. I think they just needed a warm body.

I had been working with special-needs students at the secondary level, but this was something entirely different. My new school had a growing population of preschool students with autism and severe disabilities. I knew very little about teaching students with disabilities and even less about best practices that could truly help them. So I immersed myself in learning. I went to workshops with my teachers and read as many books and articles as I could. The internet was relatively new, but I learned to use it to connect with experts in the field and bring them in, so my teachers and I could learn from them together. I became familiar with specialized teaching techniques needed to reach our students with severe communication deficits. I learned about Applied Behavior Analysis and relearned the teachings of B.F. Skinner and Ivar Lovaas. I went back to my college Psychology 101 books and then went deeper. I followed my brilliant speech therapists around and asked them question after question. I walked beside the behaviorists in the building. I learned which methods worked for our students and which ones didn't. And through all this learning, I formed a deep understanding of what was necessary to meet the needs of our students.

What I'm saying is, I was hired to be the "leader" of the building, but I became the "instructional leader" by learning every day and connecting with those much brighter than me. For real leaders, learning is a never-ending process. To be better, we must continue to learn. To be great (And isn't that what we want?), we must commit to learning for life.

When I became the principal of Slackwood School, I had just come from a supervisor position in the special-education department. I knew a lot about kids and programs specific to the needs of our special-education population, but I was not well versed in general reading or math programs. Again, I was the leader but not yet the instructional leader. I found some of our gifted teachers and spent a lot of time in their classrooms. I listened when they talked at meetings, and I'd stop by their rooms after school to talk more. I read everything I could get my hands on to learn the best practices for reading and math instruction. I went to a professional development workshop where I got to listen to Richard Allington talk about reading. And then I went to another. I read *The Book Whisperer* from Donalyn Miller, then I read *Reading in the Wild*. I went to numerous trainings about readers' and writers' workshops and read books and listened to lectures by literacy authors Kathy Collins, Kylene Beers, and Bob Probst. I attended book studies and learned more, hoping to move into the instructional leader role. The same is true for math. I had long discussions with our math specialist, and I read *Guided Math* by Laney Sammons and had the opportunity to hear her speak. I followed blogs and read books by education author and Stanford Math professor Jo Boaler. And from all these books, presentations, and expert educators, I learned what excellent teaching and leading looks like.

To be my best as a leader, I needed to be a learner. The same is true for you. And to develop a culture where learning and thinking matter, you must lead by example. Here are a few ideas for improving learning and thinking in your school:

- **Use the #EdCamp model for learning.** EdCamps are partic- ipant-driven activities where people decide what they want to learn and discuss, then split into groups and do just that. You can use this model in your staff meetings and in your class- rooms. You can even do this with your parents and commu- nity by hosting parent EdCamps, where parents are invited to come and can learn about anything in the school they don't understand or want to know more about.

- **Genius hour or passion projects are a great way to learn.** When children are passionate and excited about something, they will take learning to the next level. Why not do this with your teachers too? What drives them? What is something they want to know more about and haven't had time to learn? Give them the time.

- **Spend time learning about questioning.** I know that Bloom's Taxonomy and Webb's Depth of Knowledge seems overused, but they really help to give structure to how we need to take learning to deeper levels. Keep these resources close and post higher-order questions in the room to remind yourself to think deeply. I try to remember to ask these kinds of questions when giving feedback to teachers. I want them to really think about instruction.

- **Use current events to drive discussion**. There is a curriculum that needs to be followed for our students, but with adults, we need to be cognizant of all that is happening around us that affects our teachers and our community. Use these events and ideas to have those discussions. Make your feelings transparent on issues of importance to your school.
- **Learn something new every day**. Start a #Learn180 challenge and then stick to it. Challenge staff to learn something new each day and give them partners to hold them accountable.
- **Who is the best teacher in your building or district?** Find out what they are doing that is so special and share that. Some of it might be intuitive, but much of it can be learned.

Culture Matters: Improve Learning and Thinking

A great leader is continually thinking about ways to make his or her school better. He is listening and learning from those around him. He is connecting to those doing great things and making those things work for his school. People who are passionate about schools can't stop thinking about school. That has been my superpower.

In the end, learning and thinking are what make everything else possible in our schools. It's really what our schools are about. If schools become places that are standardized and robotic, the learning will end, and that's when we might as well shut the gates and go out of business. If we take the thinking out of learning, we crush the dreams of the future. It's up to leaders to foster great thinking and help it grow, so our world can be a better place.

Leadership Treasure Hunt
(Find This)

Who is one person in your school or district who is innovative and creative? What are they doing that you want to do? Find out!

Navigating the Seas
(Think about This)

Where do you go when you don't know something? How do you show that you value continued learning?

Charting the Course
(Take Action)

What are the next steps in your growth as an instructional leader?

Share your thoughts and ideas!
#LeadLAP

ENTHUSIASM MATTERS

As leaders, we have a responsibility to model positivity and enthusiasm. We can't expect our staff and students to be enthusiastic about things that we are not enthusiastic about. We do this by being excited about everything that school is about.

—Lead Like a PIRATE

Some days it is downright hard to get out of bed and go to school. You have a parent conference coming up, and you know it isn't going to go well. Or you know you're going to be tied up in administrative meetings for three hours—and for two hours and fifty-nine of those minutes, someone will be reading a PowerPoint to you. What do you do on days like that?

Maybe you paste on a smile and look forward to a long run or workout afterward, dreaming of those endorphins flowing through your body. Maybe you listen to loud music in your car all alone. Whatever your method of dealing with the stress, challenges, or irritations of work, you know that when the lights go on, you have to "bring it." From 7:30 in the morning until 5:00 in the afternoon, your attitude shines a light on everything you do, and people will follow your lead. That means enthusiasm matters!

Let's get back to that parent-teacher conference you were worried about. I've found the best thing is to greet the parent with a big smile and a warm handshake. Once seated, start off the conversation with at least three to five compliments for the student and give real examples of times they were golden-hearted or showed tremendous leadership skills. Oh, and don't forget to thank the parent for sharing their wonderful child with you. Then, when it's time to share the challenges, the parent will be more likely to listen and be supportive. Be direct, but instead of speaking in the negative, speak in the positive. You can say, "We're working on helping Johnny keep his hands to himself." Or, "We've developed a picture chart to help with Samantha's organization. Do you have any other ideas to help her?" Tell the parent your ideas for supporting their child through the difficulties and enthusiastically assure the parent that together you can make it happen. These conversations are easier when the parent can feel your love for their child. You become a team with one goal in mind: helping the student succeed.

Enthusiasm for our schools and our teachers can be seen in all that we do. When leaders and teachers are positive and energetic, that excitement can be seen on the faces of the students as they enter the building or classroom. Most children start school with excitement and a little apprehension. It's our job to keep building up their natural enthusiasm and keep their energy for learning high.

You can also feel it when there is a lack of enthusiasm at a school. In these schools, students get off the bus or move through the halls with what appears to be a sense of dread. The staff drag themselves out of their cars in the morning and shuffle into work. With a complete lack of excitement, mediocrity reigns. It doesn't have to be this way! Enthusiasm is a mindset, and as Dave Burgess says, "You have to bring *now!*" The question is, what are you going to bring that is an enemy of mediocrity? How are you going to put smiles on the students' faces and generate excitement in your staff each day?

Fueling your school's culture with enthusiasm starts with you; you are the one who can make the difference. The first and maybe most important way to build an enthusiastic school is to model enthusiasm for learning and growing. Show excitement every time a student works hard to achieve a goal. Celebrate each time a teacher takes a risk in her lessons and tries something new. Celebrate mistakes and failures and help people see how to use them. Help them to learn through reflection and improvement. When I see a teacher using a new technology that was modeled in a staff meeting, I make sure to acknowledge it and celebrate it. When I see a child go back and look at her mistakes and change her answers, I celebrate it. When I see the perseverance and grit in the classroom or outside, I rejoice.

I have to say, it's not hard for me to be enthusiastic about our school and the entire learning process, but some days the daily grind can get you down. On those days you go into music class or into the gym and participate along with the kids. When you see their enjoyment, you immediately change your attitude. You become one of them and let the children lead you in *their* joy.

In *Teach Like a Pirate*, Dave Burgess says, "By lighting yourself on fire with enthusiasm, you become a beacon of bliss amidst a bastion of boredom and banality." As the leader of the school or the teacher in the classroom, you must make every teacher and every child know that what is happening right now in their school or classroom is the most important and amazing thing that is going to happen to them today. They must feel it in their bones. You want the students and staff to know that the enthusiasm you show is about them and that you are excited to be with them.

Some days, just for fun, I'll bring the megaphone with me to morning bus duty. Besides using it to make the first morning announcement over the PA system ("It's 7:45, and it's time to begin our day!"), I use it to announce the students as they get off the buses. Usually we have multiple buses unloading at the same time, but I'll be out there with the megaphone saying, "Welcome to Slackwood, Johnny, glad that you are here today!" or "Here comes Susie. Looks like she's got on some new shoes!" I do this to start the day on a positive and upbeat note. Kids may step off the bus tired and sleepy, but when I'm out there high-fiving them and calling out their names, they wake up. They get excited because they know I'm excited to see them!

My school is more than one hundred years old, so there are a lot of history and traditions in our building. We actually have one of the original school bells that was used to start the day. Guess what? I sometimes take it outside and ring it to welcome the students. It's quite loud, and the neighbors may not really appreciate it, but the kids get a kick out of it! It's one simple thing that starts their day with a smile. Other days we play music or have the disco ball going in the hallways. Sometimes I take the bubble machine out for bus dismissal just to get a reaction out of the kids.

One day I found a mini-robot on the table in my office in a box. It was there for about a week until I finally asked if anyone knew where it came from. No one claimed it, so I put it together and began to play with it. The next day, I took the robot with me to bus duty as my assistant. It greeted the kids and gave out pencils and erasers. The students were so excited to get off the bus and see the robot rolling around. Our students who are walkers came over to see what was going on. The robot greeted them and walked them to the stairs (my robot can't do stairs). I still don't know where the robot came from, but I keep using it.

None of these activities are big things, but parents often seek me out at parent-teacher night or email me to tell me that their child really enjoyed having their name called out as they got off the bus, or that they thought the disco light in the hallway was cool. Even simple things can make the students feel excited and special, plus staff members get involved and amped up for the day ahead. Enthusiasm is a key pirate ploy for getting students, staff, and families running *into* our schools.

Are there days when I'm "just not feeling it"? Of course! And on those days, I remind myself that I am the luckiest person in the world because I get to make a difference for the kids every day. No matter how I feel, it's my job to show them how much I love learning—how much I love *them*!

Be over-the-top enthusiastic, and you'll get the same in return. Other simple ideas for showing how enthusiasm matters include the following:

- **Smile!** This is the easiest thing to do. Isn't it amazing to see the excitement of the students as they learn? If they aren't excited, you're doing something wrong. Smile and be happy about the learning that is going on in your school. Get excited about the fact that you get this opportunity to inspire greatness!
- **Join in.** When you see something fun or amazing going on, join in. If I walk into a classroom, and they're doing a movement activity of dancing, I quietly join in. One of my kindergarten classes marches around the room while singing "America, the Beautiful" each morning. If I walk in during that, I get in line and march.
- **Never be afraid to look silly.** I wear different hats and costumes daily. If I forget to put on a hat before going out for

bus duty, the students will remind me. They look forward to seeing what Mr. Billy has on today. They look forward to seeing what crazy thing I'm going to do. All too often, especially at the secondary level, the teachers and school leaders don't put themselves out there. But showing your silly side is one way to connect with kids. So make those connections! Get the students talking about you. It's never a bad thing to have the students think you are a little crazier than they are.

- **Greet parents and the community** with an enthusiastic slogan or saying. When someone asks, "How's it going?", your answer should be, "Never Better!" Or as I like to say about my school, "It's all good in the 'Wood'"—Slackwood, that is.
- **Enthusiastically cheer for your students' and teachers' successes outside of school.** When you share their successes beyond the school walls, you are creating a family environment that shows you truly care.
- **Start the day with music and dancing.** It's okay. Get your school a disco ball. Every school needs one.
- **Ride a bike or a skateboard** through the halls delivering messages and mail.
- **Go out on the playground,** play games, and get on the equipment with the kids. There's nothing better than going down the slide or playing catch with some of your students.
- **Take the kids out into the snow.** For some of our students, it's their first experience with snow. Keep some cheap sleds available. Build a snowman.

Culture Matters: Boost Enthusiasm at Your School

Whether you are playing music for the teachers and students when they arrive, you set up a disco ball in the hallway, or you just smile and welcome each student and staff member. As the leader of your school, you must show that you are happy and enthusiastic about being there. Every. Single. Day. The staff and community look to you to be the one to set the energy meter high. We must show how grateful and lucky we are to be part of the most amazing profession in the world. It's our job to get our students excited about walking in those doors every day. We can only do this if we are excited too.

The staff and community look to you to be the one to set the energy meter high.

Leadership Treasure Hunt
(Find This)

Who puts a smile on your face daily?
Thank them!

Navigating the Seas
(Think about This)

When was the last time you heard laughter coming out of a class so loudly that you had to go see what was happening?

Charting the Course
(Take Action)

How are you going to bring more joy and enthusiasm to your school or classroom?

Share your thoughts and ideas!
#LeadLAP

A WORD ON CULTURE
AN ADMINISTRATOR'S PERSPECTIVE

As I walk up the #KindnessMatters steps that lead to the doors of Slackwood Elementary School, I begin to ask myself: Floppy, pointy, striped, fuzzy, festive, patriotic, hairy, frilly, slimy, or groovy . . . what type of hat is Principal Billy wearing today? Is he sporting his cape and superhero pajamas? Is he using KFC buckets to build castles and forts in the gym? Will I find him curled up in the main hallway display case reading a good book? My excitement builds as I wonder what awaits me on the other side of those doors. Today I (Superintendent Edwards) will be conducting an informal observation of Principal Billy.

The office staff, guidance counselor, and school nurse welcome me with a smile as the school secretary sings and dances with the children who are celebrating their birthdays. The school is buzzing with plans for the multicultural family night, SuperYouFun Day, and reading with our GrandPals. The halls are filled with colorful artwork, creative designs, and inspirational messages.

In classrooms, children huddle in comfy spaces to buddy read, collect cardboard and gadgets to build their own arcades, design their own science experiments, and use video conferencing to share their thoughts and ideas with students in classrooms across the country. Downstairs, teachers dig through data and develop plans to pre-teach, reteach, extend, and scaffold learning for students.

I grab a seat next to the Secret Society of Readers in the library and finish typing my observations notes. The sense of shared values, camaraderie, high expectations, family engagement, creativity, academic rigor, fitness and wellness, and just plain fun that Principal Billy established as the foundation for success at Slackwood Elementary School was immediately felt upon walking into the building. Take a tour of the building and you will feel it too.

—Dr. Crystal Edwards, superintendent

JOY MATTERS

*We don't always have a choice in the day-to-day work we
do, but we definitely have a choice in the way we do it.*
—Lead Like a PIRATE

S tudents are in school at least seven hours a day. Between planning for school and working in the classroom, teachers often spend eight to ten hours a day at school. Administrators devote a similar amount of time each day, even coming to school on the weekends and off days. We spend a lot of time at school, so it isn't surprising to hear people say, "TGIF!" And as much fun as the weekends are, I think we need to turn our schools into a place where people say, "TGIM!" (Thank God It's Monday.) Schools should be a place of joy—for all of us. After all, school is not just a job; it's our profession and passion.

There are so many great things happening at schools that can be turned into joyful and happy activities. In a *4 O'Clock Faculty* blog post titled "Joy is an Intervention," Trevor Bryan explains that, although we must focus on academics and pedagogy, our first priority should be to make school and learning joyful. "My friend Dr. Mary

Howard wrote these words in a Facebook post the other day. They flipped my world upside down," Bryan writes. "I always believed that joyful learning is a key to increased learning, but I never thought of it as an intervention." By celebrating Monday or the first day after break by having a New Year's party, or celebrating any other fresh start, we are celebrating the joy we feel when the "family" is back together. It's the way life is supposed to be . . . and that's a good thing.

As I read the blog post, I began to think about how school makes me feel, how it makes our teachers feel, and how it makes our parents feel. Most of all, I thought about how school makes our students feel. Joy is an emotion I feel each day when students get off the bus. I can't wait for the first day of school each year after a long summer of empty hallways and quiet. I can't wait to see the students connecting after a long weekend or a break and talking about their lives away from school. Seeing their joy and happiness brings happiness to me.

Making school a place of fun and joy for the adults in the building is a little more difficult. I believe most educators got into the business in order to really change lives and give kids hope. That is the joy in what we do. It also helps to get the right people together because they can then generate their own fun. Seeing kids take chances and learn is fun for most educators, but doing it with a great team of people makes it better. The inside jokes and the reminders about mistakes that we can laugh about make teaming and collaboration special and make the workplace more of a home than just some place we spend eight to ten hours a day.

For teachers, joy comes with the *aha* moments when a child's learning finally clicks. Joy comes when the children arrive in the morning. It comes when students experience something for the very first time. Joy comes when students bring in math problems they made up on their own the night before or they ask to share something they wrote with the class—written just because they like to write.

Joy comes when teachers see the expressions on their students' faces when they first realize they are reading.

This is where *Teach Like a Pirate* and *Lead Like a PIRATE* really hit home with me. Reading these books allowed me to open up and share the real joy I was feeling inside. I used to be the guy that kept my little inside jokes to myself and tried to remain stoic. I'm the one who said, "That's why they call it **work** and not fun." Now I'm the one causing the ruckus. It's all part of the plan to make school fun and amazing for the kids, but by doing this, I've made it fun for me . . . and that's okay. I don't want school to be drudgery for the students or the staff. I try to share this with my staff too. By modeling this, I've made it acceptable for them to have fun in their daily routines and step outside the norm to provide amazing experiences for their students, which makes school a joyful place for them. All staff feel empowered to make joyful moments and share the fun with others.

For school leaders, joyful moments can seem far less frequent. Meetings and management responsibilities aren't all that fun, which means we often must find our own joy. For me, it's at bus duty or when I spend lunch time with the kids. Nothing makes me happier than making the students laugh when they step off the bus in the morning. But many other things bring me joy. Like I said before, when I walk into a classroom and see something I modeled or shared with a teacher, my heart fills with excitement. I know my teachers are learning and growing right alongside their students. When I learn that a parent has taken our ideas and suggestions for helping his or her child, and it is making a difference for their family, I feel an overwhelming sense of happiness.

Sometimes making school a joyful place is simply about noticing and calling attention to the little things that happen every day. And sometimes our intentions and actions can create even more opportunities to experience joy; for example, a couple of years ago, with support of the district, we received a grant to put in a walking path on our school grounds. The path has exercise stations spaced around it in keeping with our school's goal to promote wellness and fitness for our students and community. This walking path has been a very positive addition to our school and play area. Nothing brings me more joy than to stop by on the weekend and see someone from our community exercising on the path or one of our kids learning to ride their bike with their parents out there. Seeing our community enjoying our school is where I find my joy. This is how I envision a school. Some of my own children learned to ride their bikes in the parking lot of my school on weekends and nights when no one was there. My children have come to work with me on the weekends and shot baskets and played on the playground. We've taken their friends with us to school after hours when the halls weren't filled with children. My kids still tell stories of the hide-and-seek games played in the school with walkie talkies while Dad was getting his work done. I know these are some moments they will never forget. For them, and I hope for all our students, school is a place of fun, community, and happy memories.

School can be a joyful place. Here are a few simple ideas for making happy memories at your school:

- **Invite students into your office or classroom for lunch**. Not only does it help build positive relationships, but spending time with the kids in a small setting is fun and can be hilarious. I keep lots of toys, fidgets, a karaoke mic, and a robot in my office so they love to eat and play. Their new favorite is my sound-effects gadget that can imitate everything from laughter to some slightly inappropriate bodily functions.
- **Open the building for play.** I know some districts have problems with this. Everything must be scheduled a year ahead of time, but do it if you can. Just pick a date and open the gym and library. Kids will come and read and play. It's awesome.

- **Play music** in the morning before the bell.
- **Bring breakfast** for the staff. Just because.
- **Do the joke of the day** on the morning announcements. Have students provide the jokes for your next day and week.
- **#CelebrateMonday.** Follow Sean Gaillard @smgaillard on Twitter. He started the Celebrate Monday hashtag and movement, and it's such a great way to start the week on a positive note instead of with dread. Find ways to start the week on fire.

Culture Matters: Increase Joy!

School is a second home for many of us. When students grow up and tell tales of their school days, I want them to speak about our school with love in their hearts and voices. By painstakingly and thoughtfully making our schools places of joy, we increase our students' chances of success. Our mission is to teach, but we must first get students to *want* to learn. We do this by making our schools joyful. By reinforcing and supporting the happiness that comes with each new idea learned or thought expressed, we are setting them up for success. As school leaders, we must also celebrate our staff members, so the excitement continues, and the flame isn't extinguished.

Leadership Treasure Hunt
(Find This)

Ask your students what makes them happy about school and then try to make that happen every day.

Navigating the Seas
(Think about This)

What is it about school that brings you the most joy? Try to make that happen daily.

Charting the Course
(Take Action)

Find that student or staff member who seems to have lost their joy and find out what you can do to bring it back.

Share your thoughts and ideas!
#LeadLAP

COMMUNITY MATTERS

We are stronger and better collectively
than we are individually.
—Lead Like a PIRATE

I'm lucky to work in a school and district in which we have students from all over the globe; in fact, we really don't have a "majority" population. It's awesome to be part of such a diverse community.

When discussing school culture, you must understand the community you are serving. When I say *community*, I don't just mean the students, families, and staff, although they are a big part of that community. I'm including the greater community—not only the people who don't have children in schools but the business owners and leaders in your area. As school leaders, we must be aware of all that is going on around us. Without a real understanding of the communities our students and their families live in, it's tough to connect with them.

The diversity of our school makeup requires that we are very careful to educate our staff about the various cultural norms of the students and families we serve. We want to respect each and every culture and their beliefs. When we don't know, we ask. People are always happy to talk about their culture and traditions.

We also work very hard to make sure people feel comfortable in our school. In my office, my secretary is fluent in Spanish and can understand three other languages. I've found that if you don't try to understand language or cultures, the families will shy away from school and not become involved. Although I don't speak any other languages, I always strive to make anyone who walks through our doors—regardless of their heritage or background—feel important. I want my school to be the place the community thinks of as warm and helpful. Having a welcoming office staff allows us to engage our families and community so they *want* to come in and talk to us. And whether it's at kindergarten orientation, back-to-school night, or during staff orientation, I make it a point to welcome everyone to the family. We are one big family, and I want everyone to know that.

Community Connections

One of the biggest and best options I have for engaging my families is through our parent teacher organization (PTO). I've been gifted with an outstanding group of parents who work with me and understand our school vision, which is inclusive of all, with an emphasis on literacy, kindness, fun, and service. Many of the activities and functions we do are initiated by the PTO, our staff, and the community. All of them build a culture of community for our students and help them know that our school is a place they are loved and welcomed.

Last year, a gentleman from our community reached out to me about a program called GrandPals, where local seniors visit schools to read with students. Although I'm always interested in practices that involve reading and literacy, I was a little skeptical about the follow-through from this group. I directed him to our assistant superintendent to get all the volunteer permissions needed to come into our schools and work with kids. Well, wouldn't you know it, they followed through, filled out the proper forms, and all got fingerprinted. I was forced to figure out what to do with them. Scheduling weekly times is tough because the student schedules are packed, so we decided that this group of ten seniors would come in every Wednesday at 11:30 for our kindergarten lunch. I had my teachers pick a few students from each class and sent home permission slips to their parents. When the first week of the program arrived, I was still skeptical. Of course, all of the GrandPals arrived early and were waiting in the office. I brought them to our library, where my librarian had set out a big pile of hand-picked books they could use with the children. Some brought their own books, while others sorted through the pile, picking books that were new to them or ones they remembered reading to their own children.

Since it was lunchtime for our kindergarteners, I had them get their lunch and then walked them to the library. I assigned each one a GrandPal (Some GrandPals had two or three students.). Introductions took place, and while the students were eating, the seniors interacted and read with the students. It was amazing to watch. The students ate, laughed, talked, and listened as the GrandPals read to them. As I escorted the kids back to their classes after lunch, I asked them if they wanted to come again next week and got a unanimous "YES!"

The next day, a few of those kindergarteners came up to me in the lunchroom and asked, "Is today Wednesday? Can we go read with the old people?" Later a few parents called to ask why their child wasn't included. Each week our students and their GrandPals experienced a time of celebration of joy and love. This program continued again into this year, meeting with more and more kindergarteners who love seeing their GrandPals. I'm not sure who got more out of it, the GrandPals or the kids. I know for sure that none of the students will ever forget their connection with those senior citizens from our community. It brought a smile to my face to know that our five- and six-year-olds were building connections with our community in ways I never could have imagined.

Another way we've connected with our community is through the local colleges in our area. Our school has partnered with these colleges for a variety of projects and activities, and we take on preservice teachers from those campuses when we can. I enjoy speaking with preservice teachers about qualifications and interviewing to help them as they move forward. By connecting with these colleges, I have found some amazing teachers.

Collaboratively working with Slackwood Elementary School truly inspired me to teach beyond the classroom, particularly in such a warm and loving community. Watching students and their families enjoy quality time together was truly amazing! From crafts and games to pictures with Santa, witnessing firsthand how families impact education was extremely valuable to a novice educator!

—**David Eggert**, President of Rider University
Student Education Association

Our partnerships with the colleges are mutually beneficial in that their student organizations reach out to us to help with events. Last year the Rider Student Education Association helped with our Breakfast with Santa and then asked if they could put on a student game night for our kids. Both events were well attended and helped to strengthen the school community and the sense of family we try so hard to foster.

I've also built relationships with the managers at the local Barnes and Noble. Each year we schedule a night where our PTO gets a percent of the profits from the books sold. We promote an author night, or, if it's near the holidays, our teachers read at the store. This helps to make the community more than just the school. It's everywhere that we are.

There are so many things you can do to involve the school as the community. Our township has a grant-writing process where grants are awarded for ideas that serve the community. For my first few years, I wrote and was awarded grants that supported teaching English to Adults. Using that grant money, I hired a teacher to come to the school a few nights a week to teach. Then I invited our students' parents and other family members to come in and learn in our classrooms and work areas. As they learned English (which improved their job prospects), they also learned basic academic language that enabled them to help their children. It was awesome, and it continues to be a need with our families. Although we had some logistical issues and had to discontinue the program temporarily, we hope to be able to start doing this again with our families because it is a real need and benefit to our entire community.

The Road to the Reading Final Four

Another example of what one school did to involve its community in a fun literacy initiative comes from my good friend Chris Turnbull's Bear Tavern School in Hopewell, New Jersey. This activity stems from an original post by Dave Burgess titled "Repurposing March Madness." Chris and his school not only include a huge literacy initiative but inspired the entire school community to become a part of this.

During the winter of 2016, I was having a conversation with a parent. The parent asked why the school no longer uses reading logs to track reading times/pages and to compete between classrooms. I explained my philosophy on developing a love of reading in a natural way and highlighting the positive benefits of reading for pleasure, not transforming it into a task or a means to a pizza party. I explained that those types of systems could have students stop reading in the middle of a page just because time was up or might lead to a binge of reading to win a prize, then a drop-off.

I felt that I had stated my case effectively, but she then stated that each of her boys was different, and one, in particular, thrived on competition and sometimes needed an extra push.

It left me thinking. I knew that I felt strongly about timed reading, reading logs, and competitions where one class "won" and twenty-three others "lost," or everyone worked toward a tangible goal and then finished. After all, shouldn't reading be a win for everyone? But I wondered what we could do to build a school-wide sense of purpose and still encourage community, exploration, and fun. We use picture books in many of our school activities to set purpose for whole-school activities and often use them in online read-alouds during summer and school breaks to keep students connected and engaged.

We decided to go big and aim for a sixty-four-book tournament to determine our students' favorite picture book. It was very important to make families and staff stakeholders in the process and the product, but most of all, to get students excited about reading and making big decisions. We held open nominations using a Google Form and received almost one hundred picture book recommendations! Some were well known classics, others were contemporary up-and-comers, while others were more obscure and rare. It was great to see such a variety of books and so many families willing to chip in ideas.

From there, a committee met and narrowed it down to sixty-four books. We then shared the list with families and explained the project. We gave six weeks to read as many books as possible in school and at home. (Next year we will give a bit longer.) But one other important aspect was accessibility. No student had all sixty-four books, and families had varying resources to get to the library, bookstores, etc. So we asked staff who owned some of the books to bring them in so that we had as many of the books on hand at school as possible, but we committed to recording a community member reading each of the sixty-four books and posted them on YouTube. This turned out to be one of the most rewarding aspects of the project, though the most challenging. We reached out to staff members, parents, central office personnel and Board of Education members as well as the police chief, mayor, fire fighters, and more. The logistics of recording sixty-four read-alouds was tough and sometimes required me driving to locations to meet people if they were working, but we got it done! We provided families with a sheet that had all sixty-four titles and links to a special read-aloud for each.

Our committee filled in the brackets and we distributed them to students and families. There was quite a buzz around which books would advance. We paid special attention to reminding students that everyone has favorite books for a variety of reasons and that our favorite books can even change over time, so if a book was eliminated, it didn't mean that it wasn't good because there was something special about all the books that were nominated.

Our first round of voting started the Friday before the last full week of school before Spring Break. We had students hand-vote in each homeroom and teachers fill in the data using Google Forms. We made a form that was multiple choice and had a picture of each book cover for each matchup. The teachers projected the forms on their Smartboards, and kids loved it. We narrowed sixty-four books down to thirty-two, then thirty-two to sixteen using the same format. One of the most fun aspects was a giant bulletin board of the brackets in the cafeteria where students could follow the progress of the tournament. They were so excited to watch it unfold.

When we got to the round of sixteen, we had each student vote independently on Chromebooks for grades two through five. We used iPads for voting in kindergarten and grade one. It was easy and really fun to do. Seeing the pie charts that Google Forms produced and then sharing the results was thrilling each day. I must admit that some close votes even had me checking every few minutes until the voting was done.

We announced our Final Four: *The Day the Crayons Quit* by Peter Daywalt, *Knuffle Bunny* by Mo Willems, *Enemy Pie* by Derek Munson, and *The Book with No Pictures*, by BJ Novak. On the Thursday before Spring Break, we voted to narrow it down to two. Then we had a live read off on the last day of school before Spring Break. We had staff members read *Knuffle Bunny* and *The Book with No Pictures* in front of the whole school then had our final vote. The atmosphere was electric.

The Book with No Pictures was the champion of the inaugural tournament, but we had so many winners and so many intended and unintended consequences. Our sharing of reading was off the charts.

Classrooms were using our school-wide hashtag (#BearTavernPride) to share pictures of reading and book reviews but also reached out to many of the authors. I was astounded at how many authors replied and communicated with our students. The videos also highlighted great books and important community members. I received many comments from families who watched the videos even months after the competition was over. They were not edited or fancy, just a read-aloud, but boy, did the kids love watching them. We were also all (kids and grownups) exposed to some new books with which we had been unfamiliar. As a school, we had a common language in the book titles, and we had some lively and positive debates.

We chose picture books because they appeal to all ages, and they have messages that resonate with all our students. I did do an online book club with *Charlie and the Chocolate Factory* over the summer to challenge some of our older readers to tackle something a bit more advanced, but everyone had a great time as we created our Bear Tavern Road to the Reading Final Four. It will definitely become a tradition in our school!

Other community involvement ideas that have been supported by our families and our PTO include the following:

- **Popsicles on the Playground**—For no reason, have the families come back on a fall evening and just be together while their kids play and enjoy a refreshing treat. When it's hot, I may even get out the hose and sprinklers to cool things down.
- **Parents Night Out**—Around the holidays, we have had a three-hour parent's night out. Parents drop off their kids and can go shopping, wrap presents, or just have a quiet dinner while we entertain their children. Although the PTO has a slight charge for it, it is definitely worth it to the families. Also, it's not hard work for me. I usually get a couple of teachers to help me, and we set up some fun stations and then finish with

a snack and movie. To be honest, and I've said this often, I could just open the doors and let the kids run around for three hours, and they'd have a blast.

- **Multicultural Pot Luck Dinner**—This may be my favorite event (not just because of the food), and it's organized entirely by my staff and the PTO. We set up the cafeteria tables and put serving tables along the front. Each family arrives dressed in their culturally traditional clothing and carrying some of their favorite dishes to share. I enjoy watching our families and children interact and just relax with each other. We've played games and given away prizes, but we don't have to. The food and the sense of community and sharing are enough to get people excited about this event.

- **Memoirists**—We put an emphasis on reading and writing at our school because we want students to understand the importance of those activities in our daily lives. A couple of years ago, my librarian told me about a local senior center that has a group that gets together and writes their memoirs. They discuss writing strategies and the process and share stories. My librarian then asked if I would be interested in having this group to our school and share with our students. Of course! This has been a wonderful activity that connects our students with the community and helps instill a love of writing.

- **Celebrations**—We invite families to attend our celebrations; for example, at each of our character education assemblies, we honor students who have exemplified that character trait in one way or another. Their parents are invited to attend the assembly. Our school counselor also tries to identify a parent, teacher, or another community member to be recognized in front of the entire school for their character or contribution to the school.

- **Clap-in/Clap-outs**—When new students or staff join us, we hold a clap-in where all the "experienced" staff and students greet them by cheering and clapping as they enter. We do the same for our third graders as they leave us. On the last day of school, we line the halls and cheer and clap for them as they get ready to move on to the next school in the district. Those students who are moving or staff members leaving also participate. We want them to know they are valued and will always be part of our school "family." When everyone is cheering you on as you walk into school for the first time, you feel like a rock star. When everyone is cheering you on when you walk out of the school for the last time, you feel appreciated and feel like you've made an impact.

- **Send Hunger Packing**—My school counselor works with the local food bank to write a grant each year that allows us to supply our neediest students and their families with food for the weekends. Since 2011, we have sent home more than 12,500 bags of food.

- **Parades and Celebrations**—We always participate in the Memorial Day Parade as a school. Each year, a Slackwood contingent proudly carries our banner while marching down the streets. We want to be represented and show our pride. It's important to be seen out in the community.

- **Game Nights**—Get out some good, old-fashioned board games and invite families to come play. It's a night away from the TV and really connects us with the community.

Culture Matters: Build Community

When we work to connect our school with the entire community, we build a culture of inclusiveness. The only way we can do this is to open our doors and let people in. Share the greatness that is going on and be transparent. When we say yes to understanding and involving our entire community, it changes the way our school feels and the way we work. Our purpose becomes bigger than just the children in front of us at the moment. Our purpose becomes empowering our students to make a difference for the community and the world.

Leadership Treasure Hunt
(Find This)

What ideas from this section could you use
in your school or classroom?

Navigating the Seas
(Think about This)

What are ways you can get your families and
community more involved in your school?

Charting the Course
(Take Action)

How can you involve the community in holidays
and special days in your school?

A Word on Culture
A Student's Perspective

Slackwood School is a special place to my family and me. I went there from kindergarten to third grade, and it was a place where I really *wanted* to go every day. Part of why I loved being at Slackwood was Mr. Billy always letting teachers and students try new things, which made a very different and unique experience for me and my peers. For example, my kindergarten teacher, Ms. Cook, had the idea to move up to first grade with my class. Mr. Billy said, "Let's try it," and Ms. Cook and my class loved it. Mr. Billy is always saying, "Let's try it," and it makes me feel brave, like I can try something new.

Slackwood is a very diverse school, and Mr. Billy makes everyone feel welcome and important. This school celebrates its diversity with special events, such as the multicultural night. At the multicultural night, you can bring traditional clothes and food from your culture, and I always learned something new about a different culture. Another thing I loved about Slackwood was that parents play a big role in the school. Not only were my parents involved, I got to know other parents, and that made me feel more connected to my community. Slackwood is an amazing school, and it helped make me brave and confident. Now I'm ten, and though I'm at a new school, Slackwood is a big part of me.

—Zoe Snellings, student

CELEBRATIONS MATTER

*Be relentless about seeking out and
nurturing each person's greatness.*
—Lead Like a PIRATE

Throughout the year we celebrate our Pillars of Character (Trustworthiness, Respect, Responsibility, Fairness, Caring, and Citizenship) by honoring our students who exemplify these character traits. We also try to celebrate adults in our lives who show these characteristics. Our assemblies occur first thing in the morning so as not to interrupt the day. On this day in January, we were celebrating our Caring Pillar. We have a preschool group of kids that ride in on a special bus in the morning, and they need extra help and support. On this bus is a very special bus assistant who goes above and beyond in caring for our kids. We invited her to the assembly under the auspices that some of her students were being honored, which they were. More importantly, we wanted to celebrate her. Once all the students were recognized for their accomplishments, we called her to the front of the room and thanked her for all she had done for our kids. We made sure that the parents there understood how she made the bus ride special for these students each day and how the parents of these children raved about her caring nature. She was so surprised by this celebration that she welled up with tears. I know it is something she will always remember and be grateful for. She didn't expect it, but she now has become a member of our family. People know her story, and they all wish their child could ride her bus.

It is important to celebrate the effort and work of your staff and students. People like to be appreciated and relish discussions and praise for great work. If you don't believe it, check out a teacher's desk or wall near their desk or even on their door. You'll find notes of appreciation and celebration. We've learned that feedback helps to drive growth, so we must continually celebrate the good, as in good work and effort towards improvement.

I didn't always understand the need for celebration and reinforcement, because I am intrinsically motivated and very competitive in my drive to be the best at whatever I do. I didn't know that I needed a pat on the back every once in a while because I didn't much care for what others thought. I was pretty sure I was on the right track. As I read more and learned more about leadership, it became clear to me that I needed to do a better job of "filling buckets." It's true: Celebrating the great things that happen to you or go on in your school raises everyone's energy. Celebrating is one way we demonstrate that schools can and should be places of joy and fun.

So celebrate! Sing, dance, and make a ruckus! Cheer for the small wins and party for the big wins because schools should be thought of as places of celebration.

Celebration recognizes all the effort that goes into teaching and learning. It can be as simple as giving positive one-on-one feedback to someone. Or when needed and appropriate, celebration can involve public announcements that call out specific students or teachers for their great efforts. Celebrations of learning should feature student work and, when possible, involve family members. We know that students, at least elementary students, enjoy showing off to their families. Actually, I'm pretty sure all students want to know their hard work is being recognized and celebrated—even if in public they pretend it doesn't matter. It is important, when holding public celebrations of learning, that every student has someone to share their work with. If a parent can't make an event or public celebration of learning, make sure you connect with them and "be their adult" who celebrates their work. Invite their previous teachers to the celebration and make sure these children are being recognized.

There are literally dozens of days and ways you can celebrate your students, teachers, school, and learning. All you need to do is pay attention and stay connected, and the ideas will hit you in the face. Speaking of hitting in the face, one of my favorite days is March 14, Pi Day! On Pi Day, my math specialist holds a contest to see who can repeat Pi to the most places. As you know, Pi goes on to infinity, but I've had second and third graders repeat Pi to seventy-three places. Wow, that's a lot! What they win for repeating 3.1415926 . . . is the chance to hit me in the face with a pie in front of the rest of their peers. You can imagine the enthusiasm and excitement for this activity. And we're celebrating math. How cool is that?

Another great celebration occurs on May 4. Although I didn't really get it the first time I heard, "May the fourth be with you," but May 4th is *Star Wars* Day (Get it?) All kids—big and small—love to come dressed in their *Star Wars* attire and celebrate with lessons and thematic activities that feed their passions.

The school calendar provides so many opportunities for celebration. In our school, we have "The Week of Respect" in early October, during which we talk about kindness and respect, being "upstanders," and the prevention of bullying. Also in October through mid-November, we participate in the Global Read Aloud program started by literacy expert Pernille Ripp. During this six-week period, schools and classrooms make global connections by reading (or listening to) a book. What a great way to celebrate literacy and show global relevance. There are so many ways to celebrate learning, fun, and books on the calendar; all you need to do is look. There are things like Global School Play Day, World Read Aloud Day, Read Across America Week, Dr. Seuss's Birthday, and even Teacher Appreciation Week, to name a few. Use all these identified days to celebrate in your school. You can find ways to make every day memorable, but these are days identified on the calendar that will help us celebrate our teachers, our students, and our learning.

We also love to celebrate the arts. The talents and skills of the students really shine as we showcase student artwork, concerts, and drama performances. I'm always amazed at how our art and music teachers bring out the amazing talents of our students in these events. They find special skills and talents in our students that make our students stand out. I love concert days and art show days. Even though these are a lot of work, the events give our students and our school another way to show our larger community what we can do. These types of celebrations of students' special skills really make a difference in building your school culture and bringing pride in the community.

More Student Celebrations

- **Celebrations of Learning**—Book fairs, reader's theater, and poetry reading help build a culture of learning and keep everyone excited about growth.
- **Heritage Festivals**—In our diverse society, it's important to share and celebrate our cultures. We do this by learning

about all cultures and traditions as well as celebrating our differences and our similarities.

- **The Beginning and End of State Testing**—It's important to be positive and enthusiastic about the testing. If you aren't, there is no way the students will be. It's also important to celebrate the positive completion of this testing and the hard work that went into it. Don't forget to celebrate those who organized and implemented this monstrous task.

- **End of the Year**—There is so much going on at the end of the school year, but whether you do it just with your class or with your whole school, you should celebrate the learning and growth.

- **Birthdays**—As an educator, I'm not a big fan of school birthday parties because not everyone has parents who are able or capable of coming to school to celebrate. With three hundred kids in the school, it's impossible to have a full-blown party for each child, but I still think it's good to honor and celebrate birthdays. We call students down to the office to pick out a book, and we acknowledge their birthdays with a song by the office staff.

- **Monthly Character Assemblies**—These assemblies provide a simple way to celebrate the positive characteristics of our students and to remind students of our expectations. They are short, and our school counselor runs them as each teacher nominates students of character for the month.

- **Positive Phone Calls Home**—I've learned this from *Kid's Deserve It* and *Lead Like a PIRATE*: When you can call a parent while their child is in the room with you and tell them something special the child has done, you've built a bond with the entire family. These kids will want to come back for more phone calls, and their parents will be your biggest fans.

- **Holiday/Winter Concerts**—More people visit your school for these events than for any other school program or meeting. Make them great!

Remember to Celebrate Teachers and Staff Members

Honoring your teachers and staff members shows them that you recognize their hard work and commitment to your school. My goal is to celebrate in a way that doesn't feel contrived. Teachers know when you are just "Hallmarking" it, so show your sincere appreciation for and enthusiasm about the amazing things that happen with your staff and for your staff.

- **Teacher of the Year**—Each year we recognize one teacher and one education services professional for their contributions. Make sure it means something. Not everyone gets a trophy.
- **Retirement**—When someone has given their life to teaching and the district, make it special. Show them their accomplishments are valued.
- **Weekly Recognitions**—Celebrate contributions to the organization in the newsletter or at staff meetings.
- **Anchors of Appreciation**—With all that you need to do, it's important to periodically stop and just drop some anchors acknowledging the great things going on in classrooms.
- **Holiday Parties**—Although I'm not a big party guy, it's important to celebrate with your staff and be part of the festivities. When there is a party, and you're invited, you need to go and enjoy yourself.

- **Weddings and Babies**—Recognize and celebrate these great times in the lives of the staff. Also make sure you recognize when your families have new additions to their clan.

Culture Matters: Make Time to Celebrate!

Celebrations not only show off the great things in your school but also recognize the greatness of the people who make the school special. When you take the time to celebrate and share with the school community, you are acknowledging the accomplishment of a goal or at least progress toward these goals. Celebrations cause people to feel good about what is happening around them. There is both a psychological and a physiological response to celebrations that make you want to do more and work harder.

Leadership Treasure Hunt
(Find This)

What are some of the traditions and celebrations in your school?

Navigating the Seas
(Think about This)

Is there anything you wish was more of a priority to celebrate? How can you make this happen?

Charting the Course
(Take Action)

What celebrations would you get rid of if you could?

Share your thoughts and ideas!
#LeadLAP

INTENTIONALITY MATTERS

We have to be intentional in taking control of our daily schedules and prioritizing the most powerful work.
—Lead Like a PIRATE

Have you ever wondered, *What's the purpose of this?* I hope so! It's a question I ask my teachers regularly, not with sarcasm or condescension, but with the desire to be intentional about everything they do with students. So I ask . . .

What is the purpose of the work you are giving the students?

What standard are you trying to achieve?

What question are you looking to have answered?

What learning will be achieved?

What's the purpose?

When we plan our days, or when we break away from our plans, it's important to be intentional about the reasons of our actions. Relying on researched-based practices is great. And you already know

I'm a proponent of using social media to learn new ideas for teaching. But before we use any new idea or teaching method, we must have a specific purpose in mind, and that purpose must align with our stated vision and learning goals.

For example, an after-school instructor came to me one day with a concern about the homework a teacher had assigned. Her goal wasn't to belittle or "tell on" the other teacher; she just thought the homework was a waste of time because it wasn't achieving its intended purpose. It was an activity where students had to write out their spelling words in a ladder-type format.

H

Ho

Hou

Hous

House

The goal, of course, was for students to practice their spelling words. Certainly, there can be some benefit in repetitive activity like this for younger students, but the after-school teacher noticed the students were filling in the blanks vertically and were not paying attention to the spelling patterns. When I spoke with the teacher who had made the assignment, she explained that she had seen it on Pinterest and thought it was a cute way of helping the students learn the spelling patterns. The funny thing is, when done in class with the teacher monitoring the patterns and supporting the spelling patterns, this might be perfectly acceptable. As homework, this activity lost its purpose and value.

Any assigned work should be purposeful, but teachers must be especially careful when assigning work to be done independently at home. (By the way, research doesn't support using homework to teach responsibility.) Teachers need to be able to clearly identify the purpose for the work they assign—*including* word searches and work-sheets. What is the purpose? There may be a purpose to these things, but my teachers know they'd better be able to explain the purpose even if it's "I just needed five minutes to organize my next activity." I'll take that. I understand that, but don't try to make a worksheet something it is not.

Be Purposeful about Culture

As a leader, I make it my business to get into my classrooms daily. I'm not walking the halls for my health; I'm there so the students and the teachers see me and understand that I'm there—for them. I'm not there checking on them, I'm there to help and be part of the learning experience. In the business world, this practice of visibility is called "management by walking around." Although I hate using the word *management*, the practice is a good one. My purpose for walking in and out of classes is to make it clear to teachers that I'm there to support them, and they can call on me at any time. I want the students to feel that having the principal in their classroom isn't an event; it's a normal part of the way we do things in our school. As a school leader, if the kids are surprised to see you in their classrooms, then you're doing it wrong. Even kindergarteners should not be surprised or disrupted when you walk into their classroom. By the second week of school, it should be commonplace and expected. It is not uncommon to see me kneeling next to a student, helping them with their work. Often, the students are waiting for me to come by because they want to show me something they've accomplished that they are so excited about, and they feel that I need to know about it. They know that I value their hard work and their progress.

What's the purpose of calling out names on the megaphone as students get off the bus? What's the purpose of giving each student a high-five as they get off the bus? What's the purpose of wearing a different or silly hat each day for bus duty? The purpose is connecting. The purpose is creating an environment where students understand that we know them and that we're going to make school fun and exciting. The purpose is to recognize their innate value as human beings and celebrate their attendance. The purpose is to make school amazing and to get our students excited about coming every day.

> *The purpose is to make school amazing and to get our students excited about coming every day.*

Be Purposeful about Teaching and Learning

Last year, my third-grade teachers proposed the idea of becoming subject-area specialists. One teacher would teach all three classes of writing, one would teach all three classes of math, and one teacher would do all the science and social studies. Each of the three would keep their homerooms. At first I rejected this idea because research does not support this type of structure in the elementary school. I also know the value of teachers building relationships with each student, and I understand the principles of Responsive Classroom where the academic success of students is closely tied to the students' social-emotional learning.

Build a Culture of "Yes."

We talk about purpose and intentionality; I also talk about having a culture of "YES." As the school leader, there is power in the word *YES*. When we say yes to ideas that may seem a little unconventional or not "directly related to the curriculum," we give power to our staff. We give the autonomy of their classrooms and share our confidence that they are doing what is best for our students. We make it clear that we believe in them and trust them. Yes is a powerful word, and when used with intention and purpose, we can make some really amazing things happen. YES has to come with a plan, but YES builds trust and empowers our teachers and our students. Try to say yes as much as possible, and you'll see great things happening that you never expected. To put it simply, when people feel empowered, they make it happen!

My third-grade teachers were persistent and purposeful in their arguments and came to me with more details and ideas. They explained that each of them was passionate about the specific subject area and that by not having to plan for each specific area, they felt they could be more creative and go deeper into each subject. They also know that I continually talk about "My Students, Your Students, Our Students" and that every teacher and staff member is responsible for every student in the school, not just those in their classrooms. They sold me with the idea that they would have a complete connection with every third grader—even those who weren't in their homerooms. We talked through their plans, and I agreed to it with these caveats stipulated:

- They would have common planning daily and they would meet weekly to discuss progress.
- Since each teacher had different behavioral approaches, they would build a common behavioral and classroom-management system, so the students were comfortable with and fully understood the expectations.
- Class changes would occur in a timely fashion. There would be no classes waiting in the hallway while one teacher finished the lesson. Transitions would be neat and prompt.

These teachers came to me with intentionality and purpose; in fact, that's the only reason I allowed them to take this new approach. When I explained to my superintendent and curriculum director how we had "re-done" third grade, I outlined the reasons—the purpose—for the change:

- **Teacher driven and student centered**—It was the teachers' idea. As Shelley Burgess and Beth Houf say in *Lead Like a PIRATE*, "People are less likely to tear down systems they help to build." More importantly, this was their baby. They had a stake in making it work. They had their hearts in making this work.
- **Each teacher had a specific love of their subject area**—Passion inspires people to do more and work with excellence. Beyond that, passion is contagious, and students catch it!
- **Built-in movement is a plus**—Moving from classroom to classroom ensures that students are going to get up and move throughout the day.
- **Change is energizing**—Sometimes changing environments is good for our students and gives them a fresh start to the day.
- **A good use of time**—This plan ensures that students get one hour of writing, one hour of math, one hour of social studies or

science, and then one-and-a-half hours of reading. Somehow it seemed to add time to the day.

- **Deeper content**—With a specific focus, teachers can develop lessons and experiences that delve deeper into the material.
- **Better collaboration**—Built-in common planning allows the teachers to talk and collaborate. It breaks down classroom silos.

With the plan in place, and with the understanding that we could make adjustments along the way, we made it happen. And we did adjust several times along the way in the first year, but it worked. In fact, the plan fulfilled its purposes well! My teachers got to focus on their passions, and the students' learning experiences and scores improved. But so much more happened too:

- The kids made connections with each teacher. Third grade became a family of seventy-five instead of three families of twenty-five.
- The teachers collaborated more than ever before. The teacher for each subject area had to know what the others were doing, so they could help the students make connections. In the past, the teachers each did their own thing and rarely talked.
- Behaviors improved, and the teachers took responsibility for the entire grade level, not just the children in their homeroom.
- Less time was wasted in transitions, and more time was focused on subject-specific instruction.
- The teachers "knew" each student and could provide each other with ideas and targeted instructional strategies that benefited the students across every subject area.

We also made two interesting discoveries:

1. Because the kids switched for each class, they never missed out on anything. Even on shortened days or when assemblies interrupted the day, the schedule adjusted. If they had been in the same classroom all day, there's a good chance the classroom teacher may have just skipped writing for the day or skipped math for the day. That didn't happen.

2. The students actually enjoyed moving and getting to know each teacher. Their feedback was invaluable in determining whether we were going to do it again.

Be Purposeful in *Everything* You Do

Purposeful planning and a deep understanding of curriculum and instructional strategies are important in all we do because we can't afford to waste a moment of time. Our kids are too important. Throughout your day, ask yourself, "What's the purpose of this activity?" I never want to be the guy who does something "because that's been the way we've always done it." *What's the Purpose?* is my mantra when talking about all that we do.

Not long ago, I proposed the idea of eliminating snack from our morning routines. I had noticed there was a lot of wasted food in the cafeteria and wondered if snack meant the students weren't really all that hungry at lunch. Before taking the idea to my teachers, I talked about it with some of my principal friends. They were intrigued because they saw the same issue I did, not only at lunchtime but in the disruption that snack brought each morning. Some of my teachers were able keep their classrooms moving while students snacked, but others seemed to stop class for ten to fifteen minutes while snacking. *Wouldn't we save time and resources by skipping snack?* I wondered.

When I brought up the idea of eliminating snack to the teachers, they weren't too happy, but not for the reasons you might think. Some worried that learning couldn't occur when students were hungry. Others brought up a point I hadn't thought of: Snack time, especially for our youngest learners, is one of the few times (besides lunch and recess) when the students get to have conversations and talk as friends. Yes, we try to have them learn and work cooperatively, but elementary students are also still learning to socialize appropriately. Snack time provides an opportunity to learn necessary social skills. I hadn't thought of that. It's not math and reading, but it is a valuable and *purposeful* objective. Without the "What's the purpose?" as our mantra, my teachers might not have been prepared to share the thoughtful way they used this time each day.

Purposeful planning and implementation of learning is all I'm asking for. When teachers can articulate their purpose or intention—and it passes the BS barometer—then we are well on our way to deeper learning.

Likewise, our students need to understand the purpose for what they're doing. From Hattie's work on *Visible Learning*, we know that if students can articulate the purpose for an activity or their learning goal by using metacognitive strategies, that learning is more likely to occur and stick with them. "A metacognitive student sees him or herself as an agent in the learning process and realizes that learning is an active, strategic activity." Once students understand the "Why," it becomes real, and the learning makes sense to them. Learning becomes authentic.

Here are a few ways to build a culture of intentionality in your school:

- **When you see something** happening in a classroom that you're unsure of, just ask, "What's the purpose . . . ?"

- **When setting a school/classroom goal**, thoroughly research and cultivate ideas in order to clearly identify the steps necessary to achieve this goal.
- **When students are quietly working** at their desks, stop them and ask them what they are doing. It's important that they be able to explain the "what" and the "why," and if they aren't sure, the teacher helps them.
- **Check plans with a purpose**. If you're going to make teachers write lesson plans (which we all do), look for specifics and don't make it a secret. Are you looking for objectives or questioning? Make sure everyone knows your expectations.
- **Don't waste teacher or student time.** When scheduling assemblies and changing schedules, make sure your purpose is defined, and everyone knows it.

Culture Matters: Be Intentional and Build a Culture of "Yes!"

Intentionality matters. Keep the question, "What's the purpose?" at the center of each walkthrough and observation, and you'll ensure that everything you and your teachers do is on purpose.

Leadership Treasure Hunt
(Find This)

When you walk into a classroom, can
you see the learning purpose?

Navigating the Seas
(Think about This)

How will you use the "What's the Purpose?"
question to support your teachers?

Charting the Course
(Take Action)

Next time you sit in a class for more than five minutes,
and you still don't know the purpose of the
activity, will you stop and ask?

Share your thoughts and ideas!
#LeadLAP

A Word on Culture
A Teacher's Perspective

To visit Slackwood Elementary School is to visit a very special place. Slackwood School stands formidably on a corner in Lawrenceville, New Jersey, with its 113-year-old bricks holding up the walls and corridors where elementary students have been educated for decades. But the old school building holds much more than just desks, pencils, and books. Slackwood School nearly bursts with an energy and excitement that honors its history and traditions as well as celebrates the power and potential of every student who has the good fortune to come through its doors each day. Walking by the student-painted hallways, the recycled bottle cap mosaic, and the Roots and Wings Tree makes it easy to see that children are always at the heart of Slackwood. But it is also easy to see, as I touch base with my colleagues as we chat about plans for the day or discuss student needs, that it is the passionate teachers who are the soul of the school, engaging and empowering students to explore, wonder, and discover. But it is also important to recognize that a student-centered, family-involved, teacher-supported culture does not spontaneously appear, and the anchor of this community of learners is Pirate Principal Jay Billy.

Through unrelenting support, enthusiastic encouragement, and a clear focus on purpose and vision, Jay has cultivated a culture where learning, trying, risking, and growing occur every day for the children and adults in the building. Jay is a solution finder, a people person, a generous leader, and someone who is always looking to improve and do better. It is Jay's approach-ability, inclusivity, and belief in his students and teachers that make you want to jump in and embrace his work hard/play hard focus, which may mean reflecting upon a science experiment and completing a writing assessment in the morning and then constructing a cardboard robot and building a snowman in the afternoon. Every moment at Slackwood is filled with as much joyful collaboration as possible, and a deep love of learning begins to take root in all the children because of Jay's efforts.

If you do come to visit Slackwood School one day, please don't look for Principal Billy in his office, for you will not find him there. He may be welcoming the busses wearing one of his many funny hats that brings a smile to his students' faces, even the ones who may be having a tough day. He may be out on the playground teaching second graders to fold expert paper air-planes. You might have to look for him in the cafeteria where he could be mopping up spilled milk or handing out lunch. Then again, Mr. Billy could be up on the second floor shadowing a third grader so he understands what happens each day as students move between science and math. Jay leads through his hands-on hard work, seeing the best in everyone and by believing that every day is better than the day before. His positive disposition, ready smile, and openness to new ideas and experiences has certainly led to the creation of a "be more awesome" school day and a "you can do it" culture for all his students.

—Mrs. Jeanne Lane Muzi, teacher

HONESTY MATTERS

Hope on its own doesn't create change. Action does.
—Lead Like a PIRATE

My first staff meeting in my current position wasn't what I'd call "uplifting." If I had to do it all over again, I'd probably do it differently. You see, I was taking over for a beloved principal who had hired almost every teacher on the staff, and I had an agenda going in. I had worked in the district for five years as a supervisor for special education and had spent quite a bit of time in the building, so I had a working knowledge of all that went on there . . . or so I thought.

I began the meeting with a quick acknowledgment of thanks for being lucky to work with this staff and in this position. There was a lot of positivity in the room, and I quickly put an end to that by saying, "One thing I feel is important is that we make this school a welcoming school. As a supervisor, I never felt welcome as I walked into this building, and I have heard that from others too." The room got very quiet. This was my first real interaction in this position, and I had already dampened their spirits and put them on the defensive.

I went on to say that we would no longer be the "Poor us" school. We would take charge and take responsibility for what I hoped to be a great place for kids. We *were not* going to make the excuse of low socioeconomic status, and we *would* make everyone who entered our building feel welcome.

To make a long story short, I felt that I had to honestly explain how I felt when visiting the school and that others had told me they felt the same way. A few of the staff members challenged me, but I stood my ground. I'm not sure the staff understood or even knew they made people feel that way. I had to be honest with my staff. I think this honesty may have challenged them to be more careful in their interactions with administrators and parents. It also let my new staff know that making the building a positive place was important to me.

Now it's years later, and I have built relationships with all the staff. Some of the staff members I may have thought were not buying into our PIRATE culture (A PIRATE culture is about risk-taking to engage our students and community and create experiences they'll remember for a lifetime) are genuinely shy and introverted. Or I've found ways to get them out of their shells and show their "PIRATE selves" in other ways. Hopefully our discussions made them aware of how they could be perceived, and this made them more open and welcoming. Others who seemed rough around the exterior, I've discovered, are actually some of the kindest, most golden-hearted staff members you could ever have. They are super-protective of our students and our school.

Five years ago, I didn't know that. All I knew was that when I walked into the building, I perceived that I was unwelcomed. And for all of us, perceptions become reality. My goal with my poorly delivered—but very honest—speech was to change the perception of the school. I didn't want to just say that we were welcoming, I wanted that to be the reality people perceived when they walked through our doors. We've worked hard to become the school that I'd hoped we would. And I believe, now, when people enter our building, they instantly know they're in a place filled with love and kindness.

Be Direct. Be Kind.

Honest conversations are essential if you want to change your school's culture—or even just the attitude of one person in your building. And when you really want something (or someone) to change, you can't dance around the issue. Avoiding hard conversations only ensures that what you don't want will continue; for example, I once worked with a staff member who was amazing with kids and perhaps one of the most knowledgeable educators in the district. The problem was, I disliked being around her because of her negativity. I avoided her because I didn't want to listen to her negativity and woe-is-me attitude. Finally, one day when she was complaining about something, I simply told her I avoided her outside and in the hallways, and I told her why. I just blurted it out because I couldn't go on listening to her complaints, and I knew she needed to hear it. I said something like, "You know I really appreciate the work you do here, but it is really hard for me to be around you. And I know that others feel the same way."

She was flabbergasted, to say the least. She hadn't realized she came off that way, nor did she deny her negativity once I pointed it out. Our honest conversation changed everything. She consciously engaged me in positive ways. After that, I noticed others engaging with her more. Honest conversations, especially those that occur in a space of established respect and trust, can help relationships grow. Sometimes the direct approach is the way to go.

When working with parents, honesty is crucial. Yes, you always need to share positive remarks about children with their parents, but you also need to make sure parents understand the challenges their children have. As with your staff members, building trust is a crucial first step if you want your honesty to be well received. That means you *must* know the kids. All the kids. As a parent, I've gone to parent-teacher conferences where I've thought, *They don't even know my kid!* After that, I didn't listen to anything else that was being said. When parents know that *we know* their children, we have credibility with them. They'll then be more likely to listen when it's time to have tough conversations. They will rightly perceive that we want to make school better for their child. While you're at it, avoid jargon. Education language and acronyms can often confuse the issues. Be honest and explain yourself so parents can understand. If they don't understand the first time, explain it again differently. It's our job to help their children become the best they can be. Teachers are the experts, and most parents want to know the "real deal" when it comes to their children, but to hear it, they need you to share in an honest, kind, and loving way.

Provide Honest Feedback

If your teachers don't know the target or don't know that they are off target, how will they get better? In *Lead Like a PIRATE*, Shelley and Beth talk about "Captain-Directed" conversations. "Captain-directed conversations are the ones you have when you realize the teacher really needs your help". These can be the most difficult, most important conversations we have as leaders. Whether it's helping people refocus on the right objectives, correcting methods, or putting an end to unacceptable behaviors, captain-directed conversations steer people back to the desired course. Sometimes those conversations are formal, but they can be informal and brief and still get the point across; for example, I heard a teacher yelling as I walked by her classroom one day. I try to put myself in my teachers' shoes, and I know students can be frustrating. But I heard the same thing the next period and again later in the day. I made it a point to stop by the teacher's room after school and ask her if everything was okay. She looked up at me from her desk and said, "Sure, why do you ask?" It was then that I said, "I heard you yelling a couple of times today, and that isn't normal for you. I just wanted to make sure there isn't something bothering you." Although she didn't acknowledge that she had been a little too loud, the conversation clearly delivered the message that I was watching; it also showed her I was concerned for her as well as for the students.

Occasionally it's the captain who needs a conversation; sometimes my teachers give me the direction. When a teacher says, "I heard that I should stay away from you today" or "I can tell we have a sub problem," I know that I'm giving off a vibe that I don't really want in my school. Even students, who as we all know can be *very* honest, can direct the conversation. When a student says something like, "I said hi to Mr. Billy, and he just walked by me," I know I need to recalculate and change my attitude. Sure, there are problems that need to be fixed, but those moments of honesty let me know I need to refocus on the problem and not take out my frustrations on those around me.

Demonstrate That Honesty Matters

- **When you see something, say something.** If you see something that doesn't make sense, it is often better to ask about it than to make an assumption. Most of the time, the conversation causes change, even if the staff member doesn't acknowledge the reason for the criticism or feedback.
- **When working with parents, it's always best to be transparent.** Make sure they are never guessing what you're about.

That way, when it's time to have difficult conversations about their children or even their own actions, there is no doubt about where you are coming from.

- **When you don't know something, it's okay to say so.** People will respect you more if you say, "I don't know, but I'll try to find out." Be sure to follow through.
- **When you set a goal and don't reach it, don't make excuses.** Look at the data, look at your people, and figure out why you didn't get where you wanted and how you're going to fix it.
- **Honestly assess your own performance.** When your staff knows you hold yourself to a higher standard, they will support you and help build you up.

Culture Matters: Be Honest

Honesty is a necessary part of improving our schools. We need to be honest with our teachers, staff members, parents, and ourselves. People won't improve if they don't know they need to. When something isn't working, or we get feedback from others that says it's time to change, we need to pay attention and take action. Honesty in schools really matters!

Leadership Treasure Hunt
(Find This)

Recall a time or situation where your boss or leader didn't give feedback because of how he or she might make someone feel, and it had a direct effect on student learning. What should have happened?

Navigating the Seas
(Think about This)

What is one thing you wish a co-worker or colleague did differently that you believe would make your school or classroom better? Can you tell them? Will you?

Charting the Course
(Take Action)

Be honest with yourself. Name one thing you could have done better this year. How are you going to fix that?

Share your thoughts and ideas!
#LeadLAP

EVOLVING MATTERS

Changing culture requires changing the conversations.
—Lead Like a PIRATE

I'm known in my district as the "Just Do Your Job!" guy. Everyone who knows me knows that I'm all about getting *it* done. More than once, I've heard my superintendent say, "We know how Jay stands on that: *Just do your job!*" I even kept the phrase written on my whiteboard until one of my teachers suggested that I add the word *well to* the end: *Just do your job well!* It was a good addition.

I expect that when people come to work, they're there to do their jobs and do them well. Now, to some that sounds a little too businesslike and very impersonal; in fact, it sounds that way to me. But I don't want to be known as heartless and impersonal, which is why I've learned to be intentional about building relationships and trust with my staff. I've also learned that it's easier to say, "Just do your job," when people understand the real you behind the words. My teachers know that I'm not cold and hard-nosed. They understand that I am passionate about our work, and that passion drives my high expectations.

All of this has to do with *evolution*: the gradual development of something, especially from a simple to a more complex form. To evolve as leaders, we must be humble and open to criticism. We must show that we don't know everything. Once you do that, people are willing to help. I'm a work in progress; I believe all teachers and leaders must continue to be learners and growers. As we learn new things and meet new people, we become an amalgam of every experience we have, and as we find better ways to do things, we become better at our jobs. As Maya Angelou said, "Once you know better, you do better." That must be the goal of every member of our school community. To embrace change. To embrace what we know as better practices and take the risks necessary to strive for greatness.

Evolution involves learning and taking risks. We must be willing to imagine there is a better way and then be willing to search for it. As I did when I moved from one school leadership position to the next, we learn through reading. We learn through attending workshops and conferences. We learn watching others. We learn from our experiences and mistakes. Most of all, we learn from our connections. In *The Writing on the Classroom Wall*, Steve Wyborney talks about connections as his first and maybe his most important written understanding. We connect one-plus-one, and we know it equals two. We see our teachers take their ideas and make them work, and we make the connection that voice and choice works for them, so it probably will work for their students. We see how important it is to connect with our colleagues and learn from what they are doing because in doing so, we can make better educational decisions.

What Ideas and Practices Can You Evolve?

Book studies are common amongst educators. We have had several that I feel have benefitted our staff. The problem with book studies is that not everyone joins them. Often it's the same people that continue to want to learn and grow in this way. After reading the book, *No More Independent Reading Without Support* by Debbie Miller and Barbara Moss, I felt that message was so important that every one of my teachers should read it. But I didn't want to burden them with the thought of reading another book during the school year or setting up book study times. My solution: I sent out an email daily with one paragraph that I had highlighted from the book. Since I highlight most of my professional reading, it was really simple. Each morning I sent out a quick email with one highlighted section, making sure it wasn't too long for them to read. Staff got used to opening their email each morning and seeing it (and hopefully, reading it). Instead of asking my staff to commit to reading a book and participating in discussion meetings (more time), I asked for a minute a day. They appreciated the information as much as they appreciated that I didn't ask for more of their time. The next evolution of this idea for me is to use Google Classroom to share the ideas. I'm doing this right now, and the teachers appreciate the morning snippets of information, often responding or bringing it up in conversation.

More Ideas and Thoughts for Evolving as an Educator and Leader

- **Be a swimmer, not a lifeguard.** On your district professional development (PD) days, sit at the table and learn with your team.
- **When you don't know something, find out.** Always be willing to ask, research, and learn.
- **Whenever possible, present PD.** Talk to your staff, to other schools or districts, to anyone that will have you. When you can teach something, learning has really occurred.

- **Read books, blogs, and articles**. There are so many great ideas and educators out there. You can learn something every day.
- **Go to EdCamps.** Making connections with other great educators and seeing new things is an amazing way to grow and evolve.
- **Make a plan for change.** Change can be exciting, and it is crucial for growth. But it is hard for people, so it's important that everyone knows the why, the what, and the timelines.

Culture Matters: Evolve!

Greatness is a moving target. As educators and leaders, if we are not evolving, we are standing still—and that means the world is passing us. By being learners first, we guarantee that our students are getting the best of what we have to give. As the world continually evolves, so should we. We need to make sure that what we offer our students is not only the best for today, but for tomorrow as well.

Leadership Treasure Hunt
(Find This)

Think about something that is tradition or has been in place for a long time in your school. Is it still meeting its purpose? If not, how can we change it without "breaking the tradition?"

Navigating the Seas
(Think about This)

What educational truisms have you pushed aside because you now know better? (Example: Don't smile until Christmas.)

Charting the Course
(Take Action)

How would you like to see education change and evolve in the next five to ten years? How are you going to start the (r)evolution?

BEING A CONNECTED EDUCATOR MATTERS

Being the organizational leader can be lonely and difficult.
With technology, we no longer have to go it alone.
—Lead Like a PIRATE

I wasn't always good at sharing or connecting with others. I used to be the guy who just did his thing, not talking to or worrying about what others did. I still don't care much about what people think about me, but I've learned that there is a world of knowledge out there I want to access.

In 2011, I took a district workshop on how to use Twitter. During that PD, I made a Twitter handle and followed the people who were there to learn the same thing. At that time, I didn't really see the relevance of social media, especially Twitter. I had a Facebook account, so I could make sure my own kids were behaving online, but I never really posted anything. After that original session about Twitter, I don't think I even opened my account again until 2013. I thought

Twitter was for news and movie stars. I didn't care what someone was having for dinner, and I surely didn't care about the Kardashians.

In the summer of 2013, I was at the National Association for Elementary School Principals conference in Baltimore, Maryland. For some reason, I decided to stay and hear the closing keynote by Todd Whitaker. I had heard of him, and I might have even read one of his books but didn't know that much about him. During his talk that day, he said, "If you aren't on Twitter, you are missing out on some of the greatest professional learning there is." I really had never thought about using Twitter to learn. So as he was speaking, I logged into my Twitter account from my phone and began to follow him. I returned home, and each morning while I was waiting for the gym to open, I'd open my Twitter account to see what Whitaker had tweeted. I also followed many people with whom he was connected. Suddenly, I found real value in the platform. It is where I discovered interesting articles others had shared. I "favorited" the ideas I liked best so they were easy to find and share with my staff. The more people I followed, the more I learned—every morning! I was hooked! At a conference the next year, I heard author and leader George Couros reinforce my newly discovered belief that, "If you are not on Twitter, you are in danger of becoming irrelevant!" Wow! Later I read a post from Couros (which I discovered by following him on Twitter) in which he explained that if you are on Twitter, you have a "Higher Chance of Becoming Great" (bit.ly/HigherChanceofBecomingGreat). Mr. Couros shared, "Isolation is now a choice educators make. We have access to not only information, but each other. We need to tap into that." I've learned that having this 24/7 access to greatness is invaluable to my growth and the growth of our school.

Being connected matters! I have a lot of great teachers in my school; some are connected, some are not. The good thing is, those who are not yet ready to take the dive into social media still reap the benefits from those who are connected online. We share with our colleagues and learn daily. Because I have chosen to get connected, I have had the opportunity to meet so many great educators from across the country and around the world. These aren't just names in my newsfeed; they are real people whom I can reach out to when I need help. Learning from and with others has empowered me to grow as an educator.

Through the connections my teachers and I have, our students have had the opportunity to visit with numerous authors—in person and via Skype and Google Hangouts. Authors respond to classroom tweets about books and reading. They answer questions and interact with our students. All these experiences make the learning more authentic for our students.

Skype and Google Hangouts have also opened the world to our staff. We can now do professional development and learn from experts without leaving our building or even our home. We've held Saturday sessions where staff comes at their own leisure and learn through a nationwide Google Hangout. Matt Miller, the author of *Ditch That Textbook* and coauthor of *Ditch That Homework* ran a free nine-day professional-learning conference where some of the best minds in education shared their practices and tools via Google. All teachers had to do was log in to watch and learn. I can't tell you how valuable these types of learning are for all educators who want to be better. These are opportunities we wouldn't have had if someone in our building wasn't connected.

Connect for Fun *and* Learning

Technology empowers our schools and classrooms to connect with people we may never meet in person. Mystery Skype is one amazing experience that connects educators and classrooms around the world. It's an experience that changes the ways students can learn about other cultures by allowing them to visit classrooms across the country or around the world.

I first learned about Mystery Skype on Twitter and shared the idea with my staff. I thought Mystery Skype would be an authentic way for our students to learn about geography, gain map skills, and authentically connect with students from other places. A second-grade teacher in our school liked the idea of trying Mystery Skype, so she decided to use it in her classroom. Amy is a risk-taker who embraces messiness and student-led classrooms. I connected her to some of my friends who were willing to do a Mystery Skype with her class, and she read through Paul Solarz's directions for the activity in his book *Learn Like a PIRATE*. She explained the ideas to her class, assigned students jobs, and practiced them. She then set up her first Mystery Skype session. I can't tell you everything ran smoothly because it didn't. There were technology issues, and there were sound issues, but the kids eventually had a blast and connected with another class in Missouri. They loved it so much that she did more . . . and then more . . . and then more.

The best and coolest opportunity for Amy and her students came when a group of teachers from Georgia asked Amy and her students to share their Mystery Skype experiences and resources during a district PD day. We didn't have a day off, but that didn't matter. Amy had her students teach these teachers via Skype how to do the Mystery Skype. They were so organized and professional, and you could feel their pride as they talked to these teachers. I was so proud of them, and they were so excited to get to *teach* teachers. It was amazing. All because of making connections. Imagine the conversations they had with their parents at home when asked, "What did you do in school today?"

Another great opportunity came last year when Amy was looking for #MysterySkype partners outside of the United States. Because I'm part of the #BFC530 PLN, I know a school leader in Kenya. We set up a Skype session with his school in Kenya at eight in the morning our time so we could get them before leaving for the day. Our kids sang songs with and learned from their peers in another part of the world. What made this session even more special was that Amy had a new student from Africa who spoke very little English. The activity helped her make great gains with this student. Amy has since helped other teachers in our building to develop a love of the Mystery Skype sessions.

Mystery Skype Resources

Learn Like a PIRATE author Paul Solarz shares great Mystery Skype resources in his book and on his website:

- psolarz.weebly.com/how-to-set-up-and-run-a-mystery-skype-session.html.

Ditch That Textbook author Matt Miller has great Mystery Skype directions in his book and on his blog:

- ditchthattextbook.com/connect/.

Microsoft has a whole community of people to connect with who are willing to share and learn with your classrooms and schools. Search the hashtag #mysteryskype on Twitter to find thousands of people who want to connect.

All three of these resources give you a plethora of ideas on how you can use Skype or Google Hangouts to connect with the world.

Become a Connected Leader

Connecting comes in two ways: You connect through social media and then you follow or engage because of like ideas or differing opinions and discussion. You can also meet someone and then stay connected because you want to continue the relationship. If you've read *Lead Like a PIRATE*, you know that one of my best friends in education is Beth Houf, coauthor of the book. We met at a conference in 2014, and we've been able to stay connected through social media and Twitter. I continue to learn from her every day.

Brian Fanzo once wrote, "Social media won't replace a handshake. But social media done well will change the first meeting from a handshake to a hug." This is so true. I can't tell you how many friends I have who share this sentiment and how many people I've met face-to-face for the first time who feel like long time buddies. Here are a few more ways to get connected:

- **Share ideas and articles** you see on social media, stating where you found them. This will encourage others who are learners to become involved.

- **Follow and share your school hashtag** and Twitter address. Make sure to tag your superintendent even in daily tweets and messages.

- **When you go to conferences and EdCamps, make it a point to meet some of the people you follow.** Introduce yourself and have a conversation. There is nothing more invigorating and inspiring than connecting with those who are on the same bus.

- **Being connected helps your classes and your school.** You can bring authentic learning opportunities to your students that otherwise might not be available.

- **Learn how to use Skype and Google Hangouts** to share with those either inside or outside your district. Skype with authors and business people not only to see what they are doing but to share what your students are doing.
- **Use Google Hangouts or Skype** to hold a staff meeting or to have a guest speaker at a meeting.
- Hold trainings in your district on how to use social media.
- **Work with your PTO and families,** so they understand the importance of digital citizenship and media literacy.

Culture Matters: Get Connected

Having a connected culture in your school matters. It opens your school and your teachers to the world outside your district. It gives you people with whom you can share ideas. Being connected gives you a family where your ideas are welcomed and your individuality is encouraged. Because of being connected, I learn every day, I laugh every day, and get better every day.

The other quote I love about being connected is this one by International Speaker and author Kevin Honeycutt: "To have thousands of fellow minds in your pocket via mobile devices is to have an immensely unfair advantage over humans who think alone." Once you build this culture of learning and becoming better, you find there are people out there so much smarter than you (not hard for me) that really love to share. I've probably learned more on Twitter and social media over the past few years than I ever learned in school . . . and then I share it with my staff.

Leadership Treasure Hunt
(Find This)

Find someone in your building who is not connected. Share resources you've gotten through your social media connections.

Navigating the Seas
(Think about This)

Take part in an educational Twitter chat like #LeadLAP or #TLAP and connect with some new people.

Charting the Course
(Take Action)

Start a district or school hashtag that features great teaching if you don't already have one. If you do, challenge teachers to share via the hashtag.

Share your thoughts and ideas!
#LeadLAP

RELATIONSHIPS MATTER

Nothing leaders do matters much without the
trust of their teams and communities.
—Lead Like a PIRATE

I didn't always understand the necessity of relationship building—I'm the "just do your job" guy, remember? I have always enjoyed working alone and am internally driven. Now I know that my failure in my early years as a leader to devote time and energy to building connection and trust with those around me ultimately kept me from making a bigger difference in the schools in which I worked.

It's not that I don't like people; I do! But as an introvert, it takes me time to get to know people. Once I'm comfortable and familiar with people, I come across as likable and trustworthy, but if I'm not intentional—particularly about first impressions—I can come across as distant or uncaring, and that's the last thing I want!

Not long ago, one of the teachers (also an introvert) in my building asked if I remembered the first time we met. I didn't, but I did remember that, although she was a talented teacher with years of experience, we did not initially connect well. She went on to tell the story of her first impression of me. Apparently, while I was working as the supervisor for special education, we had a meeting about a student. When she walked into the room and was introduced to me, she said I didn't even look up and acknowledge her. *Ouch*! That hurts! I can't imagine being like that, but I do know that sometimes when I become hyper-focused on a task, I block out everything and everyone else. I can imagine how unenthusiastic she felt about working with me when she heard that I was named the principal of her school. Don't you think she probably shared this story with her colleagues? Her negative first impression of me likely influenced the way others in the building felt toward me. And what must she and her colleagues have thought when I delivered my speech at our first staff meeting about becoming a welcoming school? Perceptions become a person's reality, and she perceived me to be self-centered and rude. We have a great relationship now, but when she told me the story, I apologized profusely. I sincerely want people to feel important, cared for, and even loved. But her first impression of me was that I didn't care about her enough to even acknowledge her presence.

Thankfully, as I've continued to learn and evolve as an educator, I've come to understand how essential relationships are in our schools. Teachers know that it's possible to have a thousand positive interactions with a student, but the one time you lose your cool or mistreat them, you've lost them—perhaps forever. It's hard to undo some mistakes. The same is true between leaders and staff. For our schools to thrive, we must be intentional about building trust, showing we care, and making connections that foster a spirit of "we're in this together."

Let people talk. Listen well.

One key to forming strong relationships with staff and students is taking the time to talk to them. More importantly, taking time to listen with intention. When we listen to understand, we can then have a better feel for each person's situation. Listening well allows us to develop our empathetic skills. Showing empathy and understanding builds trust, and trust is the heart of every relationship and every successful school.

> *Showing empathy and understanding builds trust, and trust is the heart of every relationship and every successful school.*

As leaders in education, we have so many opportunities to learn more about the people we work with and the students in our schools. I'm lucky enough to get into classrooms all day and see teachers doing great work. I do my best to positively recognize the good teaching that is going on and the hard work of our students. It's one thing to be invited to celebrate birthdays and special events with staff members, but it's another thing to really find your fit in your school. In *Lead Like a PIRATE*, Beth and Shelley say, " . . . the treasure is being invited into *real* conversations about teaching and learning." Some of the best conversations I have had were in those moments right after school ends for the day or in the summer while teachers are setting up their rooms. I learn so much about teacher's professional passions as they prepare their rooms or clean up from a long day. I think these are the times when the teachers' minds are clear, and they are excited about what is yet to come or getting ready for the next great day.

One of the best ways I have found to get to know someone, be it a student or adult, is to watch them while they work. Listen to them talk and interact with others. Teachers want to feel like you know them. Students want to see you react when they try hard and do something amazing. Your willingness to pay attention and acknowledge their effort and greatness helps to forge a bond that makes people want to be with you and work with you.

Relationships begin the moment you meet a person, and they grow through every interaction. When you talk with young students, get down on their level—physically—and talk with them. In middle and high school, listening to them talk about what's important to them, rather than just talking at them, shows them you care. Above all, be authentic. Kids can tell when you're putting on a show.

> ## Above all, be authentic. Kids can tell when you're putting on a show.

Make sure you have fun with them, and every once in a while, play on the jungle gym or swing on the swings. If your students are older, make sure they see you at events. Even better, make it a point to interact with them in a positive way. Simple conversations and intentional moments can go a long way toward gaining trust and getting to know kids.

I love walking into a classroom and sitting next to a student or helping a student who is struggling with a math problem. I'm at my best and silliest in the lunchroom where I can sit next to kids, either at the tables or on the floor, as they finish and wait to be dismissed. When I worked as a vice principal at the secondary level, my favorite times of the day were bus duty and being in the hallways between classes. This is where relationships were made with brief conversations and positive interactions.

A few words of caution: If a student confides in you, you must keep their confidence (unless the child is in danger or others are to be put in danger). Respect is earned during difficult times. Trust can be quickly lost if you speak carelessly. Watch your words; try to never embarrass a student with a silly quip at their expense. Make sure your words always build people up rather than tear them down.

Ideas for Building Relationships with Students and Teachers

- **Be present.** Join classes for their morning meetings.
- **Be an example.** Model the morning meeting during a staff meeting using all components. The morning meeting in the classroom is designed to engage children to start the day and then set them up for success. It fosters classroom community. You can do this with staff too. Have a message up when staff enter the meeting. Start the meeting with greeting. Allow staff to share important and relevant things happening in their lives, then include a fun activity like dancing or Simon says.
- **Drop LeadLAP anchors.** Let people know about the good things you see happening in their classrooms. Drop them a note letting them know you noticed and you appreciate them.
- **Brag on people to their loved ones.** In *Kids Deserve It!*, Todd Nesloney and Adam Welcome share the idea of calling staff members' significant others and thanking them for sharing their awesomeness or calling their parents and sharing something great the staff member did.
- **Give teachers books that relate to their practice.** Each year, for teacher appreciation, I give teachers books, but I make sure

they mean something. They're usually books I've read. I highlight parts I feel will be particularly relevant or inspirational to that teacher. It takes time, but it's worth it.

- **Share reasons for becoming an educator.** Do this at a meeting and then discuss how your teachers feel about their work.
- **Play ice-breaker activities at meetings or in classrooms.**
  - **Truth or Dare.** Obviously, you need to monitor this one, but it's fun for all, and you really can get to know your people.
  - **Snowball fights.** Write one thing no one knows about you on a piece of paper and then crumple it up. Throw the "snowballs" around the room for thirty seconds, then have each person pick up a snowball, read it aloud, and try to figure out who it is.
  - **Balloon pop.** Write "getting to know you" questions on small strips of paper and put them in balloons (one question per balloon). Blow up the balloons and stick them on a dart board. Staff throw darts and must answer the questions they get or trade it for a new question.

Ideas for Building Relationships with Families

- **Attend sporting events and concerts.** When students and families see that you care enough to show up at events that aren't school related, you've taken a big step toward building a family.
- **Have Q&A nights.** Many parents don't understand the workings of the schools. They want to know why you put their child in a specific class or made the schedule the way you did. If you are transparent in your decision making, you can easily answer questions and build relationships.

- **More positive phone calls home.** Call to tell parents about something special their child did. It has a better impact if their child is with you in the room.
- **Celebrate family milestones.** When there's a birth, adoption, job promotion, or other accomplishment, send home a note of congratulation.
- **Be present at PTO and big school events.** At my school and many schools, the PTO or PTA organizes many great events for the students. Try to be a big part of those, and you'll not be sorry.

Culture Matters: Focus on Relationships

I can't stress enough that if you don't put in the time building relationships and trust, there is little chance of moving your building or your students forward. Relationships are bridges for success. Make time to listen to your staff and those around you. Make sure you are part of all the important things that happen in your school. Most importantly, make sure you allow the staff and community to know you and what you stand for.

If you don't put in the time building relationships and trust, there is little chance of moving your building or your students forward.

Leadership Treasure Hunt
(Find This)

What are some fun and amazing "getting to know you" activities you have seen used?

Navigating the Seas
(Think about This)

What is it that you'd like your staff or students to know about you that they might not know?

Charting the Course
(Take Action)

How can you find out more about your staff and students so you can be a better leader?

Share your thoughts and ideas!
#LeadLAP

A Word on Culture
A Parent's Perspective

Hello! I'm Chris Schafer. I've been the PTO President at Slackwood for the past seven years, and I never want to leave! It's an amazing place, and Jay Billy has everything to do with that! He's made it a place that you can't wait to get to, and you don't ever want to leave! He's created a culture of kindness and acceptance. He's sneaky too, inspiring his staff, students, and families each day without us even realizing. No idea is a bad idea (His typical response is, "Why not? Let's do it!), everyone is included, and everyone feels confident and good about themselves! We're a family!

Yes, the PTO has me at the school most days and for many reasons, but on the days when I don't have to be there, I still want to go. I look forward to leaving work and going to Slackwood. I find myself wanting to be a part of the culture constantly, whatever's going on, whether it's watching the kids paint the hallways with colorful dots (they really did that), impromptu sing-alongs in the hallway, learning the coolest things in the coolest ways, in and out of the classroom . . . our students are often outside learning or lying under their desks!

When I was in school, the principal's office was the one place you didn't ever want to go! Everyone at Slackwood wants to go to the principal's office; in fact, they beg to go, to run an exciting idea by him, say hello, eat lunch, or just see what Jay's up to . . . because it's always something amazing! My children couldn't wait for their chances to go and be a part of the greatness!

As my family's time at Slackwood winds down, I find myself very emotional each time I leave the school. Jay has created a culture that I always want to be a part of. It's a culture that my children, my husband, and I will always fondly remember. It's contagious, so I'm excited for the future of Slackwood under Jay's reign. As I said before, I never want to leave. Thank you, Jay, for changing all our lives for the better!

—Mrs. Chris Schafer, parent

WELLNESS MATTERS

Leading like a PIRATE can be exhausting. Taking time to rest is imperative to truly be your best you!
—Lead Like a PIRATE

It's difficult to be at your best every minute of every day, but that's what we all shoot for. Our students need us to be on top of our game both mentally and physically. In *Lead Like a PIRATE* there is a section called "Rest . . . Like a PIRATE." This section of the book challenges us to invest time in ourselves.

We all need time to recharge, but honestly, taking time off is extremely difficult for me. My mind seems to be constantly moving and working on new ideas related to making my school the best place it can be. Interestingly, *resting* doesn't have to mean completely shutting down.

Many of the things I've always done because I like to and because they make me feel better about myself are now called "wellness" techniques, such as making time for exercise. The gym is my oasis. I try to get to the gym at least five days a week because I really like the feeling

I have after a good workout; it's one way I take care of myself physically and mentally. Going to the gym is part of my *routine*.

For me, keeping a routine is even more important for my mental and physical health than the exercise I get at the gym. Every morning, I get up very early, grab a cup of coffee, and go to the gym. The early hour means I never feel like I'm taking time away from my family or feel the guilt about not being able to make the time in the afternoon because there is so much work to do. After the gym, I shower and head to the office. I intentionally arrive about an hour-and-a-half before everyone else. This is my quiet time. My routine continues at the office. First, I go through the paper, scanning for important news and reading about our community. But what I'm really looking for is the crossword puzzle. Doing the daily crossword puzzle is calming for me. It gets my mind working without stress. Each morning I'll spend ten to fifteen minutes on the crossword, sometimes finishing it, sometimes not. Either way, it calms me, but if I finish, I'm really looking for a great day ahead. Once that's done, I read through my emails and Twitter notifications. I've found that if I skip any of these steps of my morning routine, I feel a little off for the rest of the day. Once the school day starts, anything can happen, but by having some time to myself in the morning, I'm able to get my thoughts together and organize my day.

My routine is part of how I "Rest . . . Like a PIRATE." It's part of how I ensure my own wellness. As school leaders, it's our responsibility to promote a culture of wellness through modeling. That means maintaining a predictable and well-communicated schedule for our teachers, so they can plan and manage their own stress levels. It means going home on time each day—giving permission by our actions—to set boundaries between work and home life. And it means working smart, healthy habits into the school day.

Not long ago, we started "Wellness Wednesdays" for our staff, where there is a focus on taking care of physical health. At the morning meeting and via email, we share information and tips for wellness. My school nurse is the best when it comes to sharing fun and interesting ways to exercise and giving us great nutritional advice. We've had staff meetings on the walking path and done scavenger hunts to get people moving during our meetings. And throughout the week, we encourage people to get in those ten thousand steps.

The purpose of having a focus on wellness with our staff, beyond keeping them healthy and active, is to have them model healthy habits in the classrooms. We want our students to be healthy and active too because we know wellness contributes to their academic success. So we are intentional about modeling wellness. And, along with my PTO, my nurse and physical education teacher have hosted Family Fitness Nights and Zumba nights. Parents come with their kids and do fun physical activities along with enjoy healthy smoothies.

Ideas and Practices to Bring Wellness to Yourself and Your School

- **Reduce stress by communicating early and often.** Even if an event or deadline is well into the future, share the information with your staff. Give people time to plan their schedules. Be sure to send out reminders as the date approaches.
- Insist that parents send healthy snacks for their children. We know better nutrition leads to better learning.
- **Model it.** Try to eat well and get your steps in daily. When you have the chance to go out and play with the kids, do it. Let others see you walking and exercising.

- **Host wellness events.** Have the nurse and the physical educators, as well as all staff, have events, fitness nights, and activities that bring in the community and support the school's wellness goals.
- **Move!** Make sure teachers incorporate movement into their classrooms.
- **Incorporate yoga and mindfulness** activities such as breathing exercises and meditation into your daily schedule.

One more way to promote wellness is to practice mindfulness. Mindfulness is about being fully present in whatever activity you're involved in and not becoming overwhelmed by all that is taking place. Dan Tricarico's book *The Zen Teacher: Creating Focus, Simplicity and Creativity in the Classroom* helped me understand mindfulness in the simplest of ways. I can see that my morning routine of doing a crossword puzzle and quietly preparing for my day is part of my mindfulness habit. Dan encourages meditation, another practice—like rest—that is hard for me. What I've discovered, though, is that running and exercising bring me the same kind of peacefulness that others get out of sitting quietly and meditating.

Culture Matters: Focus on Wellness

Whatever it is that helps you to feel strong, calm, and mindful, try to make it part of your daily routine. To be fully present and available for others, we need to take care of ourselves. It's easy to get so immersed in our work and relationships that we forget we can't give what we don't possess. Make wellness a priority for yourself and your teachers, so you can all be at your best for those you serve.

Leadership Treasure Hunt
(Find This)

Check in with your PLN and find some school wellness activities that you could bring to your school.

Navigating the Seas
(Think about This)

What is it that you need to do to become more mindful in your practices?

Charting the Course
(Take Action)

How are you going to take care of yourself this year? What little change can you make to be a better person?

Share your thoughts and ideas!
#LeadLAP

PASSION MATTERS

...if you are interested in something, no matter what it is, go at it full speed ahead. Embrace it with both arms, hug it, love it, and above all, become passionate about it. Lukewarm is no good. Hot is no good. White hot and passionate is the only thing to be.

—Roald Dahl

We make thousands of decisions daily that affect students minute by minute. *Everything* we do matters because everything we do impacts the lives and learning of others. That reality makes our jobs as school leaders great! It also makes it tough. Without passion, the job is impossible.

The decisions we make are driven by our passions and beliefs. You must be passionate about making your school special and amazing, and that must drive you toward greatness. Without passion—real, deep, heated passion—we cannot truly get the best out of ourselves or others. But *with* passion, anything is possible. Passion is the spark which ignites the flame which, in turn, helps us to see the future and leads us toward greatness.

In schools where the teachers are passionate about children, you can feel it. You know it with every conversation you have and every interaction you observe. Likewise, in a school where the leaders are passionate about growing and learning, you can feel it. In those schools, there is a palpable sense of inspiration and engagement. There is a culture of passion.

I'm passionate about making my school *the* place to be and helping my teachers become the best teachers they can be. That means empowering them to discover and explore what they're excited about and giving them the autonomy to put those passions to use in the classroom. My favorite thing to say to a teacher when they come to me with an idea is, "Why not? Let's give it a shot. What can I do to help?" When teachers feel empowered to try new ideas, they often use their passions in ways that make our school better. This is why I allowed my third-grade teachers to focus on areas of specialization. They were each passionate about, and thus better skilled to teach, certain subjects. The end result of allowing them to use their strengths and passions was that our students' learning experiences improved. It was a win-win!

I'm also passionate about giving my students and their families opportunities to grow and learn in a place where they love learning and growing. One way we do that is to allow our students to share their passions and their love. Educational trends such as Genius Hour, 20% Time, and Passion Projects encourage students to explore their passions as they learn and develop valuable skills.

Share Your Passions to Share Your Learning

Because I'm continually learning, I try to continually teach. Being a connected educator has helped me not only to learn but to become more confident in sharing my beliefs and ideas. One thing

I've recently become more passionate about is public speaking. It's a skill that doesn't come naturally for me, but as I've learned to use social media platforms like Twitter to share ideas, I've learned that I really love to engage professionals in conversations about all facets of education. Since I am still a learner, I can confidently share this passion and feel comfortable listening to others who may have differing opinions. Whether it be an EdCamp or a planned conference, I really enjoy presenting and leading discussions in these arenas. When I get the time to share my passion and my thoughts about education and schools with other educators, it is truly enriching. Whenever possible, leaders should step outside their comfort zones and present to others whom they don't necessarily know. It forces you to be succinct, engaging, and thoughtful. When you work with your own staff, they might not call you out on things (although mine never have a problem with it), but when you present to outside people, you must have your ducks in a row. It's easy to present on something in which you are or may be considered an expert, but challenge yourself to present on something in which you need more information or learning. This will force you to step into uncomfortable territory and learn something so deeply that you can talk about it with expertise and experience. Think about this the next time you put in a proposal to present at a conference. Better yet, join someone on the EdCamp board and facilitate a discussion that you are uncomfortable with. That's what EdCamps are about: the sharing of thoughts and ideas.

I am particularly passionate about using social media in schools and have spoken at a number of conferences about this. It's easy for me to be passionate and comfortable speaking about being a connected educator because I'm living proof of the strength and power of social media. My staff is an artifact of my growth.

Actually, I'm passionate about almost all areas of education. I usually have to remind myself to slow down and listen well when someone wants to discuss or debate different topics in education. I could go on and on talking about best practices for reading and writing. I love to talk to college preservice teachers about interviewing and first-year specifics. Don't get me started on standardized testing. And homework, let's talk about homework . . . .

The point is, as the school leader, all your educational passions should be visible to your staff and to the rest of your school community. When I speak to parents at back-to-school night, I want them to know what I stand for. I want them to understand me and see my passion for their kids. If I'm just stoic and vanilla, how does that help me when a tough situation arises? It doesn't. I must know what's important to me—what I believe—and then I must be able to articulate my position. That's where purpose and passion meet. When I talk with families and students, they need to be able to see my passion and my confidence in my beliefs. Everyone in the school—your school and mine—should know what the leader stands for.

Case in point: At a school event not long ago, many of our students and families were out on the playground. The kids were playing, and the parents were socializing. One parent came up to me and asked about her daughter. I told her that her daughter was doing well and that she seemed to like school. I asked the mother if her daughter liked school, and she replied, "Yes, but I'd like to give you some advice." This mother went on to tell me that she felt I needed to have my teachers make the students become more serious about school by giving them more homework and sharing more websites and programs that students could work on. She was concerned that her daughter spent too much time watching TV and playing games on the iPad, typical behaviors for a nine-year-old.

I paused to gather my thoughts and then said, "I will definitely have my teachers talk to the kids about what they are doing after school. I don't have a problem with that. They should be outside playing, reading books, spending time with their families and learning on their own based on what their interests are."

The mother stared at me for a minute. I think she expected me to just agree with her. I then went on to explain to the mother about the research on homework for students in the elementary grades and that, although they would be getting some homework, it wouldn't be much, and hopefully it would be very purposeful. I shared that her daughter was a great kid who liked school, and it was my job to keep it that way and hopefully to inspire her to find her passions and help them to grow.

I could have just given this mother a cursory nod in agreement, but she happened to be talking about one of my passions, actually a couple of my passions: (1) the fact that kids need to play and (2) my anti-homework philosophy. I hope she understands what I believe and what I want my school to be about. She might not agree, but she now understands and sees my reasons (purpose) for the decisions and discussions I have.

What are you passionate about? What are your teachers and students passionate about? If you aren't sure, try a few of these ideas to help you develop and share your passions and recognize the passions of others:

- **Have your own Teach Like a PIRATE Day.** Make this a time where the teachers and you share your passions with the school.
- **Get to know your community.** We have a responsibility to understand what is important in our community. Invite community members in to talk about their lives and their jobs.
- **Encourage passion-based learning.** We know that those who are passionate are the ones who will change the world. Allow students and staff to have choice in their learning and their teaching.

- **Whenever possible, say yes to sending teachers to outside PD.** When they initiate the conversation about going to see or learn something, it's a huge benefit to your organization when they return inspired.
- Allow teachers to share at staff meetings. Allow students to share in the classrooms.

Culture Matters: Fuel Your School with Passion

In the end, passion is what fuels us. As Simon Sinek says, "Working hard for something we don't care about is called stress. Working hard for something we love is called passion." I'm lucky because I get to go to "work" every day and hopefully make a difference for everyone with whom I come in contact. Hopefully I'll put a smile on their faces and inspire them to greatness in some way. Making school great for everyone—this is my passion.

Leadership Treasure Hunt
(Find This)

You should already know what you're passionate about. Find out about the passions of the people with whom you work.

Navigating the Seas
(Think about This)

How have your passions grown over time? Did you used to be passionate about something but no longer are?

Charting the Course
(Take Action)

How are you going to share your passions with your constituents?

Share your thoughts and ideas!
#LeadLAP

INSPIRATION
MATTERS

Be relentless in seeking out and nurturing
each person's greatness.
—Lead Like a PIRATE

What inspires you? What pushes you to strive toward the next level of growth or even toward greatness?

I'm inspired daily by the things that go on around me:

When I see a great lesson in a classroom, I talk to the teacher about sharing it with others.

When I read a great article or blog post, I share it with my staff, hoping to inspire them.

When I see a student doing something kind, I snap a picture and share it on Twitter in hopes that their kindness will be mirrored or shared with others.

I've also found great inspiration at conferences and workshops. I hate the idea of being away from my building, even in the summer, but I've found that I'm refreshed and inspired upon returning from a powerful professional development event. When I can hear authors or experts in the field discuss a topic I'm passionate about, I become truly inspired and excited to come back and share. The same is true for my teachers who attend great workshops and seminars.

Unfortunately, I've also been to conferences where I didn't learn anything and wished I hadn't attended. This is why it's so important to make every opportunity for professional learning inspirational and exciting. When you have the chance to get outside of the building and the classroom, you want to make sure you get your money's worth. In truth, even at the worst events, there is always something to be gained. Maybe you met someone new to connect with. Maybe you were reminded of something you did a couple years ago, and now you'll bring that back out because it's a good time to revisit it. Even when there really isn't any relevant content being presented, you can, as Rich Czyz advises in *4 O'Clock Faculty*, take the time and open up your computer to do some research on your own. Take every professional learning opportunity and make it into something positive. Make a point to return to your school with fresh ideas—even if you must hunt them down.

One professional development event I've never been disappointed by are EdCamps. Whenever you get the chance to attend an EdCamp, do it! I've noticed that not a lot of school leaders go to EdCamps, but I do because EdCamps are awesome.

EdCamps are participant-driven conferences, often called "un-conferences," where the educators in the room decide the topics for discussion, and all who attend have the option of staying in the room or joining another discussion that meets their needs better. Negative people don't go to EdCamps. From the moment you pull into the parking lot of an EdCamp, you can feel the energy. That's the thing I love most about EdCamps: the energy you get from being there. Talk about inspiration! When I leave an EdCamp, I know that our educational system and the future of our schools are in good hands. People come to EdCamps to learn and share. They come to be a part of something that makes our profession special. If you want to be inspired, go to EdCamp. You will meet new people and make friends that will last a lifetime, and you will grow your professional learning network (PLN) in a way you didn't think was possible.

Quips and Quotes

I love inspirational quotes. I keep files of them on my computer so that I have them when I need them. Why do I do this? Because what others have said makes it easier for me to share my thoughts and provides a clearer picture of what I'm thinking. I'm inspired by the minds of those who have come before me or said things in much smarter ways than I can. I post inspirational quotes or thoughtful ideas in our teachers' lunchroom and try to change them periodically based on my feelings of what is the tenor or main theme of the building. The quotes I post are often given to me by my teachers, as they've learned to share what inspires them; in fact, I encourage them to post their own quotes. It's part of our culture to inspire and encourage one another.

Quotes can also serve as a mantra or sort of mission statement. My email tagline is a quote from Dave Burgess's *Teach Like a Pirate*: "Provide an uncommon experience for your students, and they will reward you with uncommon effort and attitude." I use this quote so that everyone who gets an email from me knows what I want from my school, my teachers, and myself. Again, I can't think of a better way to express this idea, and my hope is that by sharing these words, others will be inspired to live them out.

Share What Inspires You

A big part of my job is to inspire my teachers to keep working toward greatness and inspire the students in my building to love learning. Since I'm usually happy and excited about each day, that is how I start it. When I see amazing things happening, I call them out. When I find a new way to do something, I model it and share it. I want the kids and the teachers to know that I'm not afraid to try new things, and I don't care about conformity or the status quo. I know I've hit the mark when I see a teacher using something I've shared in a meeting or when I see a student reading a book I recommended.

Since I'm a big reader, I often share books and articles with other administrators in the district. If I see something relevant and pertinent, I share it because I want everyone to have the reaction to it that I've had. I want them to know what I know. My superintendent must hate having meetings with me because, although they are productive, she usually leaves with an assignment (a book or article) that I wanted to share with her. The great thing about it is, I know she reads them.

As educators, we know our job is not only to teach content but to inspire and engage students in learning. To give our students experiences they will take and with which they'll grow. As leaders, we must continue to talk the talk and walk the walk; you can't fake passion. I'm so passionate about being a leader and a learner, and I want my staff and those around me to feel that and be inspired by my passion. When people walk away from a conversation with me, I want them to want to learn more, be more, and care more.

As leaders, we must continue to talk the talk and walk the walk; you can't fake passion.

Ideas for Inspiring Others

- **Share the why.** Once people understand the importance of what you are doing, they become inspired to join you in the journey.
- **Share inspirational quotes.** Post them on common areas or leave them in staff member's boxes. Give inspirational books or books that have a message you want to share and have staff convey to others. You never know what will stick.
- **Sometimes you see greatness in others before they see it in themselves.** Make sure you give plenty of compliments and affirmation. Then ask them to share their story.
- **Be positive in the face of negativity.** You can't move your school forward when you've already dropped an anchor.
- **Use your PLN.** If you need to complain or just swear at someone, these are the people to talk to. Don't drag down those you directly lead.
- **Pull out that note of thanks from a former student or employee and read it again.** It will remind you and inspire you to be that person again. Your example can inspire others to want to be just like you.

Culture Matters: Get Inspired!

Whether you are inspiring others, or you need the inspiration, remembering and focusing on the *why* of what you do works to keep you motivated. If you can continually return to your *why,* you will have the strength and courage to keep moving forward and getting better. It's not for us; it's for them: those students who don't yet know the impact they can have on the world. It's for our children, in hopes that they can make this world a better place. It's for the teachers who shape young hearts and minds. The next time you need a boost, go sit with one of your students and just talk to them or watch them learn. You'll know *why* and will be "re-inspired" to be your best.

Leadership Treasure Hunt
(Find This)

Find a quote, saying, or something from your favorite
author that inspires you and post it on your door.

Navigating the Seas
(Think about This)

Are you an inspirational leader? What behaviors do you
share or exemplify that inspire others to be better?

Charting the Course
(Take Action)

What ideas from this chapter can you
bring to your school or district?

Share your thoughts and ideas!
#LeadLAP

KINDNESS MATTERS

There are three ways to ultimate success: The first way is to be kind; The second way is to be kind; The third way is to be kind.

—Fred Rogers

My school is known as the "Golden Hearted" school. When I came there, it had that name. Every year, I look at that moniker and think, *Should we try to change that or come up with something catchier?* Each year, it just seems to make more and more sense to want our students and our teachers to have this "Golden Heart" to hang on to. As the leader of the school, it's not only important to be kind but to teach and model the kindness for all. In my case, I've learned so much from those around me. I'm often so focused on the big picture that I need those around me to bring me back to what really matters. I work with so many kind and caring people who truly have "Golden Hearts" and show them every day. This is where we can and should make our biggest impact. This is what our true mission should be: helping every child to understand empathy and learn kindness so our world will be a better place.

Two boys were playing their version of keep away with a ball during recess. I stopped to watch the kids play, and I noticed the game was getting a little rough. "Be careful guys," I said. "We don't want to get anyone hurt." That's when I heard one say to the other, "Kindness matters!"

Each year, we try to have one mantra or saying that inspires us. For the 2017–2018 school year it was #KindnessMatters. I made a point to paint it on the stairs and steps at each entrance to our building. The words are posted throughout the school—on walls, doors, stairs, everywhere! I even took some holiday lights and pushed them through a presentation board poster to spell out #KindnessMatters in lights so everyone could see them at night, and people could always know what our school stands for.

Normally we deliberate and decide on the year's theme as a staff, but for this one, I was pretty direct when I announced that I wanted it to be #KindnessMatters. You see, Charlottesville happened. I don't watch the news a lot, but I was utterly disgusted by the hatred I saw exemplified in August of 2017 on the streets of Charlottesville. Where did these people learn to hate? How could this be happening in our country today? After watching the events of that horrible, riotous weekend, I couldn't sleep. I got up that Sunday morning and shared my thoughts in a blog post titled "It's Up to Us!":

It's up to us to teach and share love and kindness. It's up to us to model these things that make our country special in order that our children respect and love each other and stand up against racism and bigotry. Our children need us. Our country needs us. Let's do our job and teach kindness, equality, freedom and character. Let's be that light. Let's share that kindness. Let's stand up to hatred. IT'S UP TO US!

Modeling and recognizing positive character traits has always been part of our school's culture. In fact, our district was recognized in 2015 as a National District of Character from the organization Character.org. Our opening-day speaker in 2016 was Michele Borba, author of *UnSelfie: Why Empathetic Kids Succeed in Our All-About-Me World.* Michele's message to us was that empathy can be taught, and it's important that we make time to teach it and model it for our students. But on that August 2017 weekend, as I watched scenes of violence and hatred in real time, I was moved to make kindness our focus—our mission. Teaching kindness to the next generation is critical if our nation and our sense of humanity is going to survive. We, as educators, must make every day's mission about teaching kindness; we must exemplify it every minute. We must help our students understand the power of empathy and the necessity of seeking to understand different points of view.

Kindness in Action

In 2012, Hurricane Sandy hit New Jersey hard. Besides the massive flooding at the shore, the high winds and rain devastated the entire state. Downed trees and flooding left many without power or clean water. At the time, I lived about twenty-eight miles from school (about a fifty-minute commute) in a town that got flooded out from the Raritan River, and the power in the town where I lived was out for an entire week. Interestingly enough, some of the schools in our district still had power. Not all of them, but some. With school canceled for the week, I headed to my school to check on things and get some paperwork done.

With the downed trees and powerlines, the drive that was normally about fifty minutes took me almost three hours. When I finally arrived at the school, I was relieved to see that the power was on and was surprised (and pleased) to see so many people taking refuge in the building. Our business administrator and our district reached out to the people in the township who were without electricity. He provided buses to the neighborhoods to bring people from the rehabilitation center, senior center, and homes without power into the high school. There he and the kitchen staff provided hot meals, a place to charge technology and phones, and allowed people to take warm showers. They set up a room for kids to watch movies. They opened the gym for kids to play while the parents rested for a few hours or reached out to those who were worried about them. I saw incredible kindness that day with strangers helping strangers. I knew that kindness was important in our district, but that day I understood that the trait is really what we are about. I never felt prouder to work here.

> *Value kindness. It's easy to get caught up in stressing performance and achievement in a test-driven society. Push the Pause button periodically and listen to your dialogue. What proportion of your messages addresses achievement and performance? What about kindness and caring? If you notice an imbalance of one-sided messages, make an intentional effort to tip the scale back to stress kindness a bit more and performance a bit less.*
>
> —Michele Borba, *Unselfie: Why Empathetic Kids Succeed in Our All-About-Me World*

The best way to teach kindness is to model it. When students come to the office, we remind them of appropriate greetings, and if a please or thank you is warranted, we expect it. We make it a point to ensure people feel welcomed when they come to our school.

The best way to teach kindness is to model it.

Another way to help people develop kindness is to recognize it in others, both publicly and one-on-one. I've already mentioned the character assemblies held throughout the year during which the school counselor presents awards to children, teachers, and other staff members who exemplify the Pillars of Character (Trustworthiness, Respect, Responsibility, Fairness, Caring, and Citizenship). During these assemblies, we also honor students who have a received a Golden Heart Acknowledgment ticket. The tickets are given to students who do something special or nice for someone else even when not asked. When teachers or staff members see an act of kindness, they make note of it on a ticket and turn it into the office. Students can also submit tickets when they witness kindness in others. The tickets are all submitted secretly, and the names of the students who have received Golden Hearted Acknowledgment tickets are read over the intercom on the morning announcements. It's so fun to watch students hear their names announced when they didn't expect any recognition at all. In most cases, these students were just doing what they do: being nice! The teachers make a big deal about their students receiving these tickets so that others begin to notice when people do nice things— and hopefully follow suit with their own acts of kindness.

In her book, *What's Under Your Cape?*, Barbara Gruener uses the acronym S-U-P-E-R-H-E-R-O-E-S to define positive character traits. The first S is for service. Although we have the youngest students here, we try to promote service in everything we do. As Barbara explains, "At schools of character, every student serves, whether it's something seemingly small, like being the line leader or caboose, or a little more involved like serving on the safety patrol." We are continually searching ways to promote service-learning for our students. The best is when our students see a need and then start a movement. We've had a lot of this in our district and in our school whether it's donating supplies to the local soup kitchen, collecting winter coats for those in need, or providing care packages for military members who won't be home for the holidays. One of the most basic and charitable things our students have done is collect socks to be distributed through the homeless shelter. Simple acts of kindness and service make a significant impact on our students because they realize there are others out there who don't have many things they take for granted. Our PTO actively supports these service-learning opportunities because #KindessMatters to our entire school community.

Ways to show and recognize kindness in your school:

- **Share acts of kindness** on Twitter, Facebook, and Instagram with a hashtag like #KindnessMatters or #ChooseKind. Kindness breeds more kindness.
- **Participate in World Kindness Day activities.** Here is the website where they share many ideas: randomactsofkindness.org/world-kindness-day.
- **Be intentional about kindness.** Put service activities on the calendar around the holidays—or anytime—to emphasize kind gestures and activities. Try a month of kindness with thirty different activities that are shared with students and staff.
- **Make needs real by getting involved.** Organize a field trip to an area shelter or food bank, so students understand the importance of community involvement.
- **Praise kindness.** Recognize parents at assemblies who have shown their "Golden Hearts" in one way or another.
- **Pass notes.** At a staff meeting or other faculty meeting area, use sticky notes to write kindness notes about something you saw from another staff member.
- **Create a kindness board.** Post acts of kindness you've seen and encourage others to do the same.

- **Show appreciation.** Have an abundance of thank-you cards and various #kindness cards on hand. Make them easily accessible, so staff can use them when and where they want.
- **Leave a note.** Put thank-you notes on teachers' cars so they get them when they leave for the day. Or better yet, have the students write them and leave them for the teachers.

Culture Matters: Model Kindness

This probably should have been the first chapter in this book because, when it comes down to it, we need kindness if we are going to change the world. Teaching kindness is one of the greatest gifts we can give our students and our families. When we make our schools kind places, we make the world a better place, and that is the real reason we do what we do. It's up to us to make sure our students know that #KindessMatters!

When we make our schools
kind places, we make the
world a better place.

Leadership Treasure Hunt
(Find This)

Find those who are doing kind things in your building or in your community and recognize them for their efforts.

Navigating the Seas
(Think about This)

How can you cultivate a culture of kindness in your school?

Charting the Course
(Take Action)

From whatever position you have, how will you share your kindness with others?

Share your thoughts and ideas!
#LeadLAP

Moving On

I've evolved as a leader and an educator. Where I once tried to do everything myself, I've learned to involve others in the work and decisions. Where I used to keep my passions and excitement to myself, I now share that with others. I hope something in this book has inspired you.

When I think about what has had the greatest impact on my evolution as a leader, two things stand out: (1) becoming a PIRATE educator/leader and (2) becoming a connected educator.

By examining and understanding the PIRATE acronym, I've been able to feel confident in my decisions to take risks and try new things to improve teaching and learning experiences for my staff and our students. Making school better and instilling a lifelong love of learning are my *why*—the purpose for everything I do as an educational leader. As a PIRATE leader, my goal is to help my staff find ways to "provide uncommon experiences for our students" so they will "reward us with uncommon effort and attitude." Each day, I ask myself, *How I can inspire the teachers I work with and provide our students with experiences that will "have them running in, not out"?*

The second factor that has helped me grow as a leader involves my PLN. Being a connected educator has expanded my professional learning network in ways that were unimaginable before I began using

Twitter. I am so thankful for each and every educator who inspires me, challenges me, accepts me, pushes me, and keeps me humble. I've learned more about being an educator and a leader in the past five years from my online community than I'd learned in the twenty previous years. I know that learning and growth will continue because when things get tough, I have people who listen to me, encourage me, and help me find the right path. I will be forever grateful to Todd Whitaker and his keynote that convinced me to give Twitter a try.

If you've made it to these final paragraphs, I thank you. I hope you'll take something from this book that inspires you and use it to change, grow, and be better. That has been my goal and my mission.

Being an educator and a leader is one of the most amazing and humbling careers we can have. We are lucky to do what we do, and we must remember every day that *what we do matters!* Go out and change the world and inspire others to do the same.

Share your thoughts and ideas!
#LeadLAP

Thank You

To all the Teachers, Administrators, Students, and Families:

Each and every day, you all have contributed to my growth as an educator and a person. This book is dedicated to the "amazing and awesome" you bring to our kids daily. I am the luckiest guy in the world to be able to spend my days doing what I love to do. That is thanks to you!

To My PLN:

Who knew back in 2011 that there was such a thing? Every one of you has made me a better leader and educator. I can't imagine doing it without you.

To Dave, Shelley, and Beth:

Wow! Meeting you all has changed and enhanced my life in so many ways. Each of you has made me a better PIRATE, and for that I'm humbly grateful. Thanks for taking a chance on me.

BRING JAY BILLY
TO YOUR SCHOOL OR DISTRICT

Jay's workshops and keynote presentations help teachers and administrators thrive and equip them to improve school culture and build community:

- Educational Leadership
- Building School Culture
- Using Social Media in Schools
- Developing Your PLN
- Passion in Education
- Changing Schools
- What's Important for Teachers New to the Field
- Interviewing
- Difficult Conversations around Race and Equity
- Building a School Community
- Using Technology to Enhance Instruction.

To learn more, contact Jay:

 @JayBilly2

 jbilly455@gmail.com

BIBLIOGRAPHY

Chapter 1

Burgess, Shelley, and Beth Houf. *Lead Like A Pirate* (San Diego, CA: Dave Burgess Consulting, Inc., 2017), 165.

Chapter 2

King, Jeff, and Lopez, Damen. *TurnAround Schools: Creating Cultures of Universal Achievement.* (TurnAround Schools Publishing, 2008).

"Speech in the House of Representatives." Abraham Lincoln. June 20, 1848.

Hernandez, Donald, J. "Double Jeopardy: How Third-Grade Reading Skills and Poverty Influence High School Graduation." (The Annie E. Casey Foundation: Baltimore, Maryland, 2012).

Peale, Norman Vincent. *The Power of Positive Thinking.* (New York, NY: Prentice-Hall, 1952).

Chapter 3

Currie, Brad. Twitter, November 8, 2014, Twitter.com/TheBradCurrie/status/531071200530026496.

Chapter 4

Burgess, Dave. *Teach Like a PIRATE.* (San Diego, CA: Dave Burgess Consulting, Inc., 2012).

Chapter 5

Bryan, Trevor. "Joy is an Intervention," Four O'Clock Faculty, September 21, 2017, fouroclockfaculty.com/2017/09/joy-is-an-intervention.

Chapter 8

John Hattie. *Visible Learning* (New York, NY: Routledge, 2009).

Sarris, Natalie. "Mastering Metacognition: The What, Why, and How." ActivelyLearn.com, Feb. 23, 2017, activelylearn.com/post/metacognition.

Chapter 11

Honeycutt, Kevin. Twitter, Jan. 28, 2014, twitter.com/kevinhoneycutt/status/428151088387072000.

Chapter 16

Borba, Michele. *UnSelfie: Why Empathetic Kids Succeed in Our All-About-Me World.* (New York, NY: Touchstone, 2016).

Gruener, Barbara. *What's Under Your Cape?: SUPERHEROES of the Character Kind.* (Northville, MI: Ferne Press, 2014).

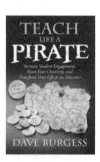

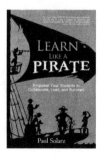

P is for PIRATE

Inspirational ABC's for Educators

By Dave and Shelley Burgess (@Burgess_Shelley)

In *P is for Pirate,* husband-and-wife team Dave and Shelley Burgess tap personal experiences of seventy educators to inspire others to create fun and exciting places to learn. It's a wealth of imaginative and creative ideas that make learning and teaching more fulfilling than ever before.

eXPlore Like a Pirate

Gamification and Game-Inspired Course Design to Engage, Enrich, and Elevate Your Learners

By Michael Matera (@MrMatera)

Create an experiential, collaborative, and creative world with classroom game designer and educator Michael Matera's game-based learning book, *eXPlore Like a Pirate*. Matera helps teachers apply motivational gameplay techniques and enhance curriculum with gamification strategies.

Play Like a Pirate

Engage Students with Toys, Games, and Comics

By Quinn Rollins (@jedikermit)

In *Play Like a Pirate*, Quinn Rollins offers practical, engaging strategies and resources that make it easy to integrate fun into your curriculum. Regardless of grade level, serious learning can be seriously fun with inspirational ideas that engage students in unforgettable ways.

The Innovator's Mindset

Empower Learning, Unleash Talent, and Lead a Culture of Creativity

By George Couros (@gcouros)

In *The Innovator's Mindset,* teachers and administrators discover that compliance to a scheduled curriculum hinders student innovation, critical thinking, and creativity. To become forward-thinking leaders, students must be empowered to wonder and explore.

Pure Genius

Building a Culture of Innovation and Taking 20% Time to the Next Level

By Don Wettrick (@DonWettrick)

Collaboration—with experts, students, and other educators—helps create interesting and even life-changing opportunities for learning. In *Pure Genius*, Don Wettrick inspires and equips educators with a systematic blueprint for beating classroom boredom and teaching innovation.

Ditch That Textbook

Free Your Teaching and Revolutionize Your Classroom

By Matt Miller (@jmattmiller)

Ditch That Textbook creates a support system, toolbox, and manifesto that can free teachers from outdated textbooks. Miller empowers them to untether themselves, throw out meaningless, pedestrian teaching and learning practices, and evolve and revolutionize their classrooms.

50 Things You Can Do with Google Classroom

By Alice Keeler and Libbi Miller
(@alicekeeler, @MillerLibbi)

50 Things You Can Do with Google Classroom provides a thorough overview of this GAfE app and shortens the teacher learning curve for introducing technology in the classroom. Keeler and Miller's ideas, instruction, and screenshots help teachers go digital with this powerful tool.

50 Things to Go Further with Google Classroom

A Student-Centered Approach

By Alice Keeler and Libbi Miller
(@alicekeeler, @MillerLibbi)

In *50 Things to Go Further with Google Classroom: A Student-Centered Approach*, authors and educators Alice Keeler and Libbi Miller help teachers create a digitally rich, engaging, student-centered environment that taps the power of individualized learning using Google Classroom.

140 Twitter Tips for Educators

Get Connected, Grow Your Professional Learning Network, and Reinvigorate Your Career

By Brad Currie, Billy Krakower, and Scott Rocco
(@bradmcurrie, @wkrakower, @ScottRRocco)

In *140 Twitter Tips for Educators*, #Satchat hosts and founders of Evolving Educators, Brad Currie, Billy Krakower, and Scott Rocco, offer step-by-step instruction on Twitter basics and building an online following within Twitter's vibrant network of educational professionals.

Master the Media

How Teaching Media Literacy Can Save Our Plugged-In World

By Julie Smith (@julnilsmith)

Master the Media explains media history, purpose, and messaging, so teachers and parents can empower students with critical-thinking skills, which lead to informed choices, the ability to differentiate between truth and lies, and discern perception from reality. Media literacy can save the world.

The Zen Teacher

Creating Focus, Simplicity, and Tranquility in the Classroom

By Dan Tricarico (@thezenteacher)

Unrushed and fully focused, teachers influence—even improve—the future when they maximize performance and improve their quality of life. In *The Zen Teacher*, Dan Tricarico offers practical, easy-to-use techniques to develop a non-religious Zen practice and thrive in the classroom.

Your School Rocks . . . So Tell People!

Passionately Pitch and Promote the Positives Happening on Your Campus

By Ryan McLane and Eric Lowe (@McLane_Ryan, @EricLowe21)

Your School Rocks . . . So Tell People! helps schools create effective social media communication strategies that keep students' families and the community connected to what's going on at school, offering more than seventy immediately actionable tips with easy-to-follow instructions and video tutorial links.

The Classroom Chef

Sharpen Your Lessons. Season Your Classes. Make Math Meaningful

By John Stevens and Matt Vaudrey
(@Jstevens009, @MrVaudrey)

With imagination and preparation, every teacher can be *The Classroom Chef* using John Stevens and Matt Vaudrey's secret recipes, ingredients, and tips that help students "get" math. Use ideas as-is, or tweak to create enticing educational meals that engage students.

How Much Water Do We Have?

5 Success Principles for Conquering Any Challenge and Thriving in Times of Change

By Pete Nunweiler with Kris Nunweiler

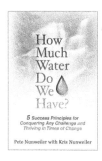

Stressed out, overwhelmed, or uncertain at work or home? It could be figurative dehydration.

How Much Water Do We Have? identifies five key elements necessary for success of any goal, life transition, or challenge. Learn to find, acquire, and use the 5 Waters of Success.

The Writing on the Classroom Wall

How Posting Your Most Passionate Beliefs about Education Can Empower Your Students, Propel Your Growth, and Lead to a Lifetime of Learning

By Steve Wyborney (@SteveWyborney)

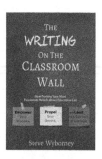

Big ideas lead to deeper learning, but they don't have to be profound to have profound impact. Teacher Steve Wyborney explains why and how sharing ideas sharpens and refines them. It's okay if some ideas fall off the wall; what matters most is sharing and discussing.

Kids Deserve It!

Pushing Boundaries and Challenging Conventional Thinking

By Todd Nesloney and Adam Welcome
(@TechNinjaTodd, @awelcome)

Think big. Make learning fun and meaningful. *Kids Deserve It!* Nesloney and Welcome offer high-tech, high-touch, and highly engaging practices that inspire risk-taking and shake up the status quo on behalf of your students. Rediscover why you became an educator, too!

LAUNCH

Using Design Thinking to Boost Creativity and Bring Out the Maker in Every Student

By John Spencer and A.J. Juliani (@spencerideas, @ajjuliani)

When students identify themselves as makers, inventors, and creators, they discover powerful problem-solving and critical-thinking skills. Their imaginations and creativity will shape our future. John Spencer and A.J. Juliani's *LAUNCH* process dares you to innovate and empower them.

Instant Relevance

Using Today's Experiences to Teach Tomorrow's Lessons

By Denis Sheeran (@MathDenisNJ)

Learning sticks when it's relevant to students. In *Instant Relevance,* author and keynote speaker Denis Sheeran equips you to create engaging lessons *from* experiences and events that matter to students while helping them make meaningful connections between the real world and the classroom.

Escaping the School Leader's Dunk Tank

How to Prevail When Others Want to See You Drown

By Rebecca Coda and Rick Jetter
(@RebeccaCoda, @RickJetter)

Dunk-tank situations—discrimination, bad politics, revenge, or ego-driven coworkers—can make an educator's life miserable. Coda and Jetter (dunk-tank survivors themselves) share real-life stories and insightful research to equip school leaders with tools to survive and, better yet, avoid getting "dunked."

Start. Right. Now.

Teach and Lead for Excellence

By Todd Whitaker, Jeff Zoul, and Jimmy Casas
(@ToddWhitaker, @Jeff_Zoul, @casas_jimmy)

Excellent leaders and teachers *Know the Way, Show the Way, Go the Way, and Grow Each Day.* Whitaker, Zoul, and Casas share four key behaviors of excellence from educators across the U.S. and motivate to put you on the right path.

Teaching Math with Google Apps

50 G Suite Activities

By Alice Keeler and Diana Herrington

(@AliceKeeler, @mathdiana)

Teaching Math with Google Apps meshes the easy student/teacher interaction of Google Apps with G Suite that empowers student creativity and critical thinking. Keeler and Herrington demonstrate fifty ways to bring math classes into the twenty-first century with easy-to-use technology.

Table Talk Math

A Practical Guide for Bringing Math into Everyday Conversations

By John Stevens (@Jstevens009)

In *Table Talk Math*, John Stevens offers parents—and teachers—ideas for initiating authentic, math-based, everyday conversations that get kids to notice and pique their curiosity about the numbers, patterns, and equations in the world around them.

Shift This!

How to Implement Gradual Change for Massive Impact in Your Classroom

By Joy Kirr (@JoyKirr)

Establishing a student-led culture focused on individual responsibility and personalized learning *is* possible, sustainable, and even easy when it happens little by little. In *Shift This!,* Joy Kirr details gradual shifts in thinking, teaching, and approach for massive impact in your classroom.

Unmapped Potential

An Educator's Guide to Lasting Change

By Julie Hasson and Missy Lennard (@PPrincipals)

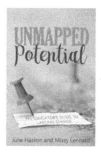

Overwhelmed and overworked? You're not alone, but it can get better. You simply need the right map to guide you from frustrated to fulfilled. *Unmapped Potential* offers advice and practical strategies to forge a unique path to becoming the educator and *person* you want to be.

Shattering the Perfect Teacher Myth

6 Truths That Will Help You THRIVE as an Educator

By Aaron Hogan (@aaron_hogan)

Author and educator Aaron Hogan helps shatter the idyllic "perfect teacher" myth, which erodes self-confidence with unrealistic expectations and sets teachers up for failure. His book equips educators with strategies that help them shift out of survival mode and THRIVE.

Social LEADia

Moving Students from Digital Citizenship to Digital Leadership

By Jennifer Casa-Todd (@JCasaTodd)

A networked society requires students to leverage social media to connect to people, passions, and opportunities to grow and make a difference. *Social LEADia* helps shift focus at school and home from digital citizenship to digital leadership and equip students for the future.

Spark Learning

3 Keys to Embracing the Power of Student Curiosity

By Ramsey Musallam (@ramusallam)

Inspired by his popular TED Talk "3 Rules to Spark Learning," Musallam combines brain science research, proven teaching methods, and his personal story to empower you to improve your students' learning experiences by inspiring inquiry and harnessing its benefits.

Ditch That Homework

Practical Strategies to Help Make Homework Obsolete

By Matt Miller and Alice Keeler (@jmattmiller, @alicekeeler)

In *Ditch That Homework*, Miller and Keeler discuss the pros and cons of homework, why it's assigned, and what life could look like without it. They evaluate research, share parent and teacher insights, then make a convincing case for ditching it for effective and personalized learning methods.

The Four O'Clock Faculty

A Rogue Guide to Revolutionizing Professional Development

By Rich Czyz (@RACzyz)

In *The Four O'Clock Faculty*, Rich identifies ways to make professional learning meaningful, efficient, and, above all, personally relevant. It's a practical guide to revolutionize PD, revealing why some is so awful and what *you* can do to change the model for the betterment of everyone.

Culturize

Every Student. Every Day. Whatever It Takes.

By Jimmy Casas (@casas_jimmy)

Culturize dives into what it takes to cultivate a community of learners who embody innately human traits our world desperately needs—kindness, honesty, and compassion. Casas's stories reveal how "soft skills" can be honed while exceeding academic standards of twenty-first-century learning.

Code Breaker

Increase Creativity, Remix Assessment, and Develop a Class of Coder Ninjas!

By Brian Aspinall (@mraspinall)

You don't have to be a "computer geek" to use coding to turn curriculum expectations into student skills. Use *Code Breaker* to teach students how to identify problems, develop solutions, and use computational thinking to apply and demonstrate learning.

The Wild Card

7 Steps to an Educator's Creative Breakthrough

By Hope and Wade King (@hopekingteach, @wadeking7)

The Kings facilitate a creative breakthrough in the classroom with *The Wild Card*, a step-by-step guide to drawing on your authentic self to deliver your content creatively and be the *wild card* who changes the game for your learners.

Stories from Webb

The Ideas, Passions, and Convictions of a Principal and His School Family

By Todd Nesloney (@TechNinjaTodd)

Stories from Webb goes right to the heart of education. Told by award-winning principal Todd Nesloney and his dedicated team of staff and teachers, this book reminds you why you became an educator. Relatable stories reinvigorate and may inspire you to tell your own!

The Principled Principal

10 Principles for Leading Exceptional Schools

By Jeffrey Zoul and Anthony McConnell (@Jeff_Zoul, @mcconnellaw)

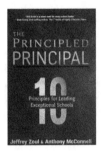

Zoul and McConnell know from personal experience that the role of a school principal is one of the most challenging *and* the most rewarding in education. Using relatable stories and real-life examples, they reveal ten core values that will empower you to work and lead with excellence.

The Limitless School

Creative Ways to Solve the Culture Puzzle

By Abe Hege and Adam Dovico (@abehege, @adamdovico)

Being intentional about creating a positive culture is imperative for your school's success. This book identifies the nine pillars that support a positive school culture and explains how each stakeholder has a vital role to play in the work of making schools safe, inviting, and dynamic.

Google Apps for Littles

Believe They Can

By Christine Pinto and Alice Keeler (@PintoBeanz11, @alicekeeler)

Learn how to tap into students' natural curiosity using technology. Pinto and Keeler share a wealth of innovative ways to integrate digital tools in the primary classroom to make learning engaging and relevant for even the youngest of today's twenty-first-century learners.

Be the One for Kids

You Have the Power to Change the Life of a Child

By Ryan Sheehy (@sheehyrw)

Students need guidance to succeed academically, but they also need our help to survive and thrive in today's turbulent world. They need someone to model the attributes that will help them win not just in school but in life as well. That someone is you.

Let Them Speak

How Student Voice Can Transform Your School

By Rebecca Coda and Rick Jetter
(@RebeccaCoda, @RickJetter)

We say, "Student voice matters," but are we really listening? This book will inspire you to find out what your students really think, feel, and need. You'll learn how to listen to and use student feedback to improve your school's culture. All you have to do is ask—and then *Let Them Speak*.

The EduProtocol Field Guide

16 Student-Centered Lesson Frames for Infinite Learning Possibilities

By Marlena Hebren and Jon Corippo

Are you ready to break out of the lesson-and-worksheet rut? Use *The EduProtocol Field Guide* to create engaging and effective instruction, build culture, and deliver content to K–12 students in a supportive, creative environment.

All 4s and 5s

A Guide to Teaching and Leading Advanced Placement Programs

By Andrew Sharos

AP classes shouldn't be relegated to "privileged" schools and students. With proper support, every student can experience success. *All 4s and 5s* offers a wealth of classroom and program strategies that equip you to develop a culture of academic and personal excellence.

Shake Up Learning

Practical Ideas to Move Learning from Static to Dynamic

By Kasey Bell (@ShakeUpLearning)

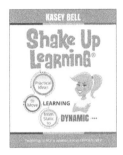

Is the learning in your classroom static or dynamic? *Shake Up Learning* guides you through the process of creating dynamic learning opportunities—from purposeful planning and maximizing technology to fearless implementation.

The Secret Solution

How One Principal Discovered the Path to Success

Todd Whitaker, Sam Miller, and Ryan Donlan (@ToddWhitaker, @SamMiller29, @RyanDonlan)

An entertaining look at the path to leadership excellence, this parable provides leaders with a non-threatening tool to discuss problematic attitudes in schools. This updated edition includes a reader's guide to help you identify habits and traits that can help you and your team succeed.

The Path to Serendipity

Discover the Gifts along Life's Journey

By Allyson Apsey (@AllysonApsey)

In this funny, genuine, and clever book, Allyson Apsey shares relatable stories and practical strategies for living a meaningful life regardless of the craziness happening around you. You'll discover that you really do have the power to choose the kind of life you live—every day.

Shake Up Learning

Practical Ideas to Move Learning from Static to Dynamic

By Kasey Bell (@ShakeUpLearning)

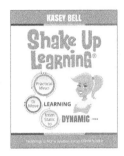

Is the learning in your classroom static or dynamic? *Shake Up Learning* guides you through the process of creating dynamic learning opportunities—from purposeful planning and maximizing technology to fearless implementation.

The Secret Solution

How One Principal Discovered the Path to Success

Todd Whitaker, Sam Miller, and Ryan Donlan
(@ToddWhitaker, @SamMiller29, @RyanDonlan)

An entertaining look at the path to leadership excellence, this parable provides leaders with a non-threatening tool to discuss problematic attitudes in schools. This updated edition includes a reader's guide to help you identify habits and traits that can help you and your team succeed.

The Path to Serendipity

Discover the Gifts along Life's Journey

By Allyson Apsey (@AllysonApsey)

In this funny, genuine, and clever book, Allyson Apsey shares relatable stories and practical strategies for living a meaningful life regardless of the craziness happening around you. You'll discover that you really do have the power to choose the kind of life you live—every day.

About the Author

Jay Billy is an elementary principal in Lawrenceville, New Jersey. He graduated from Ashland University in Ashland, Ohio, and immediately went to the University of Delaware, where he received his master's degree in physical education. In 1985, Jay became the head wrestling coach and physical education instructor at American University, where he coached and taught for seven years. In 1992, Jay and his family moved to New Jersey, where he taught at Mercer Junior/Senior High School while coaching wrestling at Princeton University (1993-1995) until moving into administration. Jay received his master's degree in educational leadership from The College of New Jersey in 1997. He first served as supervisor of behavior at the high school before moving to principal of the Joseph Cappello School in 2000.

He has worked for Lawrence Township Public Schools since 2007. He maintains his passion for leading and learning and innovative practices inside schools and classrooms by reading and working with his colleagues. Jay is passionate about making school and learning fun and engaging for everyone in the community, including Teachers, Students, and Families. He received the 2016 Exemplary Educator award from the New Jersey Dept. of Education. Jay is active on Twitter @JayBilly2, and you can often find him in his office dreaming of making school amazing and doing school differently.

CPSIA information can be obtained
at www.ICGtesting.com
Printed in the USA
LVHW04s0231160618
580898LV00007B/21/P

9 781946 444790